Praise for *Spiritual Growth*

There is no better guide for a revitalized spiritual life than Rabbi Paul Steinberg. For Jews seeking a path of compassion and openness within their own tradition, for anyone willing to add Jewish wisdom to their toolkit, if it is spiritual growth you seek, *Spiritual Growth* is your passport to a spirituality that is wide, open, and wondrous.

—Rabbi Dr. Bradley Shavit Artson, Roslyn and Abner Goldstine Dean's Chair, Professor of Philosophy, American Jewish University

Inspired by his own journey as a seeker and Jewish scholar, Paul Steinberg reveals how ancient Jewish teachings and spiritual practices can provide a powerful force for personal healing and integration.

—Estelle Frankel, author of *Sacred Therapy* and *The Wisdom of Not Knowing*

Rabbi Steinberg helps us remember to not only look up but also inward—and that the spiritual pursuit is a journey that takes effort and time. He is a voice of our ancestors, and, like our tradition, his writing transcends the moment. He speaks to the timelessness of human longing for a connection with the Divine.

—Rabbi Will Berkovitz, CEO, Jewish Family Service, Seattle

With vulnerability, humility, and intellectual rigor, Steinberg shows us that Judaism offers us a powerful response to this complicated life, and that we can go on with faith, hope, and God.

—Rabbi Sherre Hirsch, Senior Rabbinic Scholar, Hillel International, Author of *We Plan, God Laughs* and *Thresholds*

Lots of books tell us we can achieve great illumination through meditation and other spiritual practices. This book tells us how. With gentle guidance and understanding, Paul Steinberg draws on Jewish teachings and religious practices to guide us toward an enriched inner life and ways to achieve deeper connections to friends and community. This is a book that inspires and illuminates!

—Susannah Heschel, Eli Black Professor of Jewish Studies, Dartmouth College

Rabbi Steinberg articulates a vision for spiritual growth that is grounded and accessible. By envisioning "spirituality" as a process of personal integration and transformation, he provides a step-by-step guide that is attainable for people who are beginners in exploring inner work as well as more-experienced seekers who are looking for an authentic pathway within Judaism.

—Rabbi K'vod Wieder, Temple Beth El of South Orange County, Aliso Viejo, CA

Spiritual Growth

Spiritual Growth
A Contemporary Jewish Approach

Rabbi Paul Steinberg

Terra Nova Books

SANTA FE, NEW MEXICO

Library of Congress Control Number 2018963003

Distributed by SCB Distributors, (800) 729-6423

Terra Nova Books

Published by Terra Nova Books, Santa Fe, New Mexico.
www.TerraNovaBooks.com

ISBN 978-1-948749-15-2

For Rina, Nili and Liora—
May you always grow . . .
May your minds grow broader,
your hearts grow bigger,
And your spirits grow brighter.

A Note of Gratitude

Books are curious things to produce. When I published my first book in 2003, my mentor and teacher, Elliot Dorff, said to me that publishing a book is the closest a male can come to giving birth. He might be right.

Although male physiology clearly offers no equivalent experience, what I think he was getting at is the fact that a book is not merely ink on pages conveying information and thoughts. A book is the embodied result of an individual's reaching deep within himself or herself and drawing forth from the core conscious and visible elements in the form of ideas and words. Indeed, the Jewish mystics believed that words are the vehicle with which God birthed the world. Whatever the metaphor, this book certainly is born from my heart.

I also owe a debt of gratitude to several people who made this work come to fruition. First, I want to thank all the communities I have served in the past, including Levine Academy in Dallas; Valley Beth Shalom in Encino, California; and Beit T'Shuvah in Los Angeles. I have learned so much from each of these communities, and have certainly incorporated the voices of my mentors into this work, particularly Fred Nathan, Dr. Susie Wolbe, Wende Weinberg z"l, Rabbi Harold Schulweis z"l, Rabbi Ed Feinstein, Harriet Rossetto, and Rabbi Mark Borovitz. I also want to thank the current community that I serve, Congregation Kol Shofar in Tiburon, California, and Rabbi Susan Leider, who gives me continuous inspiration to be wholehearted in whatever I do.

I am also incredibly grateful to Marianne Williamson for contributing the Foreword to this book. Marianne is a national treasure and a true inspiration to multitudes. Everything she writes and says is worth our attention and consideration, and I know her voice will deepen the genuine intentions of this work.

Thank you to Terra Nova Books and the work of my editor, Marty Gerber. Marty is a *mensch*. He patiently worked with me, learned with me, and tirelessly induced from me the most lucid and worthwhile representation of both the ideas and language that meet the aims of this work.

On a more personal level, I am grateful for the support of my parents—Irwin and Pat—who are models of living big, immersive lives. My siblings Ellen, Donny z"l, Rick, and Carolann are especially imbued in my heart, as they have always given me the strength and confidence to pursue a life of big ideas. I also want to thank my friend Cantor Rebekah Mirsky for being a reader of my initial manuscript, giving me the confidence and encouragement to pursue this project.

Finally, thank you to my partner, Chloe Grey, who has continuously and compassionately encouraged me to express myself. Simply put, this work would not have been accomplished without her support, love, and encouragement.

To anyone reading, I am grateful to you. As the psalmist writes: "May the words of my mouth and the meditations of my heart be acceptable to you" (Psalms 19:14). I pray that there is something within these pages that you find meaningful and useful in your life.

Just as the hand held before the eyes hides the highest
mountain, so our petty day-to-day life hinders us from
seeing the fantastic lights and secrets that fill the world.
—*Rabbi Nachman of Bratzlav*

A man needs to love and to hate at the same moment,
to laugh and cry with the same eyes,
with the same hands to throw stones and to gather them,
to make love in war and war in love.
And to hate and forgive and remember and forget,
to arrange and confuse, to eat and to digest
what history
takes years and years to do.
—*Yehudah Amichai*

Contents

Foreword

Three times after I began my career speaking on *A Course in Miracles*, I talked with rabbis who were in the audience.

They had been curious, I suppose, to hear this Jewish woman discuss metaphysical themes using the language of *A Course in Miracles*. And each time, the scene unfolded in pretty much the same way: After hearing me speak, the rabbi would ask politely, "So perhaps we could talk?" after which I immediately reverted to my childhood brain. All they had said was, "So perhaps we could talk?" and in my head, I had heard, "Meet me in my office. NOW."

The point that all the rabbis wanted to convey was the same: Respectfully but adamantly, each in their own way said, *"You could have found it HERE!"*

The first two times this happened, I remember getting somewhat defensive. But when it occurred again with the third rabbi, a well-known Jewish scholar, I became plaintive instead. I remember blurting out with tears in my eyes, *"No one ever taught me!"*

And to his credit, he understood. I had been brought up in a conservative Jewish synagogue. I had not been a Bat Mitzvah but I had been confirmed. I remember going to Hebrew school through high school. So why had I needed to seek spiritual sustenance anywhere else? What had been missing in my Jewish education?

The book you're holding in your hands is what was missing: a deeper explanation of the spiritual themes of Judaism, lost too often amid the cultural and political issues that so often dominate the Jewish experience. As important as my Jewish identity has been to me and always will be, it was not within Judaism's theological framework that I first found my heart's path to God.

In fact, the mystical path of Judaism is as deep, as golden, as searing in its human and divine implications as is the core of any great religious or spiritual teaching. Yet I, like millions of other Jews, as well as non-Jews, did not have access for years to the universal principles that make the Jewish religion so profound. That is why books like this one are so important.

Rabbi Steinberg's story is different from mine but in many ways similar, in that both of us as young people lived the journey of the inner diaspora. We longed for the spiritual depth that being a Jew made part of our very being yet which we could not always find within our own religion. Both of us ultimately got there, we found ourselves at home in God, and have lived to speak and write of our respective journeys. Rabbi Steinberg has made a profound contribution to all of us by writing this book, providing a popular elucidation of the themes that make the Jewish call to God so beautiful and profound.

I have come to understand the history of my generation of Jews, and why in the years after World War II, there was a lack of continuity within American Jewish education. I have also come to appreciate the depth of the Jewish experience that I did receive when growing up. But while my own path has led me to not in any way discard my own religion but to teach spiritual principles based on a non-religious, non-denominational path, as a Jew I am extremely grateful for Rabbi Steinberg's contribution to both Jews and non-Jews.

The American Jew, particularly, has a historic and religious obligation to keep alive the eternal flame that burns within the Jewish soul. Why is a question I will leave to others to elaborate on. But as a Jew, as a mother, and as a citizen of the world, I am deeply aware that an understanding of the ancient, ageless, timeless wisdom of Judaism is a light unto the ages. The world is better off whenever we have a deeper understanding and experience of God, through the portal of Judaism or any other.

Rabbi Steinberg has removed a veil that too often lies across the deeper layers of Jewish thought, revealing some secrets of the heart that guide any soul in its search for God. He has given us the gift of his teaching, and through it, may not only his readers but all the world as well be blessed.

—Marianne Williamson

About Marianne Williamson:

Marianne Williamson is an internationally acclaimed author and lecturer. For the last thirty-five years, she has been one of America's best-known public voices, having been a popular guest on television programs such as *Oprah, Larry King Live, Good Morning America,* and *Bill Maher.* Seven of her twelve published books have been *New York Times* Best Sellers, and four of them were Number 1. The mega-best seller *A Return to Love* is considered a must-read of the New Spirituality. A paragraph from that book, beginning, "Our deepest fear is not that we are inadequate. Our deepest fear is that we are powerful beyond measure ..." is considered an anthem for a contemporary generation of seekers.

Marianne's other books include *The Law of Divine Compensation, The Age of Miracles, Everyday Grace, A Woman's Worth, Illuminata, Healing the Heart of America, A Course in Weight Loss, The Gift of Change, Enchanted Love, A Year of Miracles,* and her newest book, *Tears to Triumph: The Spiritual Journey from Suffering to Enlightenment.*

Introduction:
The Why and What of This Book

All journeys have secret destinations of which the traveler is unaware.

—Martin Buber

Showing up at the Saban Theater in the heart of Los Angeles on a dark Monday night was not something I would naturally find myself doing. But I did it. I was there to see Marianne Williamson, who was a sort of celebrity to me. After all, Marianne Williamson was on "Oprah!" And I was familiar with her book *A Return to Love*, and had commonly quoted her poetic refrain:

> Our deepest fear is not that we are inadequate.
> Our deepest fear is that we are powerful beyond
>   measure.
> It is our light, not our darkness, that frightens us.

So there I was, in a movie theater with about three hundred others on an overcast Monday night, seeking inspiration.

The evening started with a meditation. Marianne began by inviting us to close our eyes, to imagine a golden ball in our mind's eye, and then to follow her imagery. She expressed respect for the group and framed the evening as a most holy journey on which we were all embarking. The meditation ended, and she was present. She lectured passionately—preached really—for about forty-five minutes explicating a passage from the book *A*

Course in Miracles. Although Marianne is Jewish, *A Course in Miracles* uses a lot of Christian terminology, though in a universalistic, mystical mindfulness kind of way. The best description I could give is that it is a sort of Christian Kabbalah with a spiritual pedagogy, intended to train the mind to be more expansive and disciplined.

The finale of the evening, however, was the most fascinating part. Marianne fielded questions from the audience. She was serious and firm, never merely accepting the premise of the questioner. Sure, she affirmed each of the enthusiastic hand-raisers, yet she did not shy away from drilling into their personal motivation for asking the question. Occasionally, she even turned the question back to the asker, yet in a gentle and forthright manner, depending on the context. She also took opportunities for teachable moments about spiritual questions pertaining to work, disease, political corruption, and love. I sat there wondering what journals she must have read to be able to speak so confidently on the variety of topics presented.

It worked, though. Marianne worked, and many of us continued to show up week after week on Monday nights, for a suggested donation of $15. The audience was largely people from thirty to fifty-five years old. It was the kind of demographic that most synagogues and churches long to attract. Undoubtedly, Marianne has some name recognition, and sure, Oprah recommends her books, but the truth is that all she really did was show up and preach spiritual ideas (though not to diminish the value of doing that).

I enjoyed the Mondays I attended. Frankly, however, I had seen many people do similar things in various other settings. I would even suggest that there are a few rabbis out there who are similarly talented, knowledgeable, and compelling teachers. Still, I showed up the weeks I could. Eventually, Marianne moved her weekly lectures to Manhattan, and I curiously continued to follow her, watching a few of them via livestream.

As a rabbi and Jewish educator who also works in the business of promoting spirituality, I learned a lot from going to see Marianne week after week.

First, I should say that I gained a lot from listening to her spiritual message. She drew from an eclectic variety of resources, both traditional and contemporary, offering a very personal response to spiritual issues. Second, I learned that there is an audience for spirituality, and for spiritual solutions to life's questions. Marianne enthusiastically presented spiritual solutions at every turn. That was her purpose, and no one doubted it.

Third, I learned that the audience for this is broad in age, color, ethnicity, gender, and religion. (In fact, a few demonstrably religious Jews attended from time to time.) In other words, she was marketing to a broad target audience, and somehow in the breadth of that target, there was an inherent lack of threat to those who showed up. Indeed, her audience was not defined by any homogenous demographic but rather by the topic: spirituality. She showed me that there is an audience for spirituality, and that this audience is incredibly diverse.

I assumed at the time—perhaps wrongly—that most of Marianne's spiritual audience is characterized by a lack of religious affiliation or institutional devotion. I assumed that those attending on those Monday nights were not getting all they were seeking from a church or synagogue or mosque. Or perhaps that religious institutions represented hypocrisy or even some kind of threat to them. Undoubtedly, most folks who came those Monday nights were clearly modern and living in the secular world by all outwardly recognizable ways.

However, given the content of their questions, one can easily deduce that many of them participate in some kind of spiritual practice or philosophical exercise regimen, such as yoga, martial arts, mindful meditation, or a 12-Step program. Some may stress eating organic or vegan. Many expressed deep appreciation for the outdoors and care for the environment and animals. Essentially, from everything I could ascertain, the audience was comprised of wonderful human beings and spiritual seekers.

But I couldn't help wondering what percentage actually were affiliated with a religious or spiritual institution, since the question of the distinction between religion and spirituality was surely present for me. Certainly, the group found Marianne worthwhile, and, as a Jewish clergy person concerned about diminishing affiliation rates and synagogue attendance, I was fascinated as to how she was able to sustain her audience each week, both in person and via livestream.

Of course, Marianne has her own publicity campaign and team of people handling advertising and marketing, which helps to get the word out and draw an audience. That being said, advertising and marketing are ultimately only as successful over the long term as the product—or, in this case, the content—allows. Marianne's content is simple. First, her content is herself: an authentic human being sharing a spiritual message. She has never claimed to be a guru and has built no church nor asked for any cult following. Second, her message is universal enough to include a broad audience and yet particular enough that it can make a claim of truth and relate back to a specific text, namely *A Course in Miracles*—a text I believe many people (including me) were unaware of before they discovered Marianne.

Attending those weekly spiritual events affirmed what I have believed for many years: that despite the power of secularism in America, many people still are seeking some sort of spiritual message and connection. When I started attending Marianne's sessions, I see in retrospect, I had begun to doubt that and was becoming cynical about the future of spiritual—and certainly organized religious—life.

This doubt led me to ask: What is the spiritual message of Judaism? Are we as Jews presenting a compelling spiritual message that is both universal and yet particular enough to attract people? When we speak of Jewish spirituality, what exactly do we mean?

And do I, as a rabbi and educator, know what I believe about Jewish spirituality—as opposed to the external religious trappings—and if so, am I presenting it in a compelling way for contemporary Jews living in the modern secular world?

My Path of Spiritual Growth

The context of these questions and my experience with Marianne really speak to a macro-perspective on what compelled me to write this book. However, there also is a micro-perspective, which is my own personal journey—the unique steps that have led to where I stand today in my relationship with Judaism, as well as with spirituality in general.

For starters, I had a sort of eclectic Jewish upbringing. I went to Reform Hebrew school for a few years, then to an ultra-orthodox Chabad day school. I had a Conservative bar mitzvah and grew up with many non-Jewish family members, including siblings. (My mother was raised as a Catholic and had a marriage with children before converting and marrying my father.)

After my early Jewish education and bar mitzvah, I basically bought into the premise that I had "graduated" from Judaism. This was a most beneficial approach, of course, considering my teen-age life which consisted of doing only things that I wanted to do when I wanted to do them. Thus, from what had been quite-intense religious training, I transitioned into a "twice-a-year Jew" (i.e., I showed up for Passover seders and the High Holidays).

In college, however, I found myself experiencing a very intense existential crisis. I simply did not find any meaning in my college experience or where it might lead me. Nearly simultaneously, my parents were touched, and their Jewishness re-inspired, by the teachings of Zalman Schachter-Shalomi and Renewal Judaism. The confluence of our experiences led to my parents' helping me take time off from school—with the sole condition of my going to Israel instead. I agreed with little fuss and landed as a volunteer at Kibbutz Mizra, which, interestingly, was notoriously nonkosher. I spent much of that year working in a meat factory making hams. Yes, hams! And I loved it. (How they do hams in Israel is an entirely other story and book.)

Ultimately, my time on the kibbutz accomplished what my family and I had hoped for: I was truly restored by the experience, with my sense of purpose renewed and my Jewish identity reinvigorated. I returned to my hometown of Tucson and ventured off to finish college and pursue a more spiritually grounded life.

Fast forward two years. There I was pursuing a master's degree at the Graduate School of Education of American Jewish University in Los Angeles, studying alongside rabbinical students and surrounded by rabbinic professors. It did not take long for some of those professors to begin encouraging me to apply to rabbinical school. Ambitious about the suggestion but yet a bit ambivalent—the way I seem to make most decisions, even to this day—I went for it.

Rabbinical school had a profound effect on me. It was both inspiring and terrifying. On one hand, I was exposed to incredible material and teachers, which both humbled and stimulated me. On the other hand, I never felt as if I completely fit in with the other rabbinical students. Many of them had what I saw as a more-typical Jewish upbringing, and knew how the Jewish community (particularly the Conservative movement) worked. I did not know much about the structures and institutions of the Jewish community, which meant that I did not totally understand how rabbis functioned in the field. That also meant, therefore, that I did not know how I would function in the field as a rabbi, and I was afraid to appear ignorant and inauthentic by asking.

Though rabbinical school may have affirmed my ability to perform, the problem was that my performance often felt like exactly that: a performance. I began to experience what psychologists refer to as an "Impostor Syndrome."[1]

That is, I did not entirely feel worthy of the title of rabbi which I would soon acquire. The entirety of Jewish tradition seemed as if it would be balancing on my shoulders, because a rabbi is seen as a "symbolic exemplar" of the wisdom and morality that Judaism represents.[2]

Therefore, upon finishing rabbinical school, I vowed to myself that the one thing I would never do is work as a pulpit rabbi in a large congregation. With such a visible public role, a pulpit rabbi seemed to me to be the most obvious expression of myself as an "impostor." Instead, I stayed close to my strengths as an educator, and served as director of a day school in Dallas for four years. There, along with not having a pulpit from which to preach, I found a way to combat my feeling of inadequacy by writing books about the Jewish holidays. Writing was not only a wonderful outlet of expression but also allowed me to continue my study. The books received some good press, and my national market value ascended.

Nevertheless, a few years later, despite everything I had vowed, I took a position at a large suburban synagogue. I seemed to have either forgotten why I'd avoided synagogue work in the first place or justified it to myself because of the location in Los Angeles or the salary hike. So there I was during the fall season of my first year on the pulpit, delivering a High Holiday sermon to scores of people—the epitome of what I had previously wanted to avoid for feeling like an impostor. Soon, I found myself restless, uncomfortable, and insecure, and I was not entirely sure why. I felt as if I had a lot to do all the time, even when I didn't and actually had time to relax and enjoy life. Only later, I realized that work was my mechanism for coping with the feelings of fraud, inadequacy, and anxiety. I believed (albeit subconsciously) that continuous hard work was necessary to "earn" my place.

I accomplished a lot during those years, but at the same time, I became a depressive workaholic, and gradually both a workaholic and an alcoholic. It took a few years, but my alcoholism finally exploded my world, and I was forced to go into treatment. The shame I experienced was a living hell. Everything I had worked so hard for, and what had begun as a path set with good intentions, seemed to have been lost entirely. Moreover, my family was breaking apart, and my relationship with my three children was going to change forever. Just as the psalmist said, "From out of the depths, O Lord, listen to my cry,"[3] I too began to desperately call out to God for help.

This was the most devastating thing that could ever happen to me, and yet, in hindsight, the best thing that ever happened to me. Treatment—the 12 Steps and making *teshuvah* (repentance and amends)—gave me a freedom I'd forgotten I even had. I woke up to the fact that I have more choices about my life than I had realized. All that I had been experiencing was feeling trapped, boxed-in, and enslaved. But the truth is that the narratives and boxes I'd created for myself kept me unaware of the freedom that also was available. I realized, with a lot of help from wonderful people, that my slavery was largely self-imposed and that I could begin again as a human being, a man, a Jew, and a rabbi in the way that I believed was most true to myself. I certainly did not need to be a workaholic and alcoholic to cope with the stresses and pain of life.

It was then that I became interested in a new kind of spirituality, informed by what I was learning from the 12 Steps, psychotherapy, self-help literature, and many sages (both Jewish, including Marianne, and non-Jewish) whom I had never before taken quite so seriously. Everything I learned became a way to rethink my spirituality and integrate it with my Judaism, which was always something I'd felt I was inadequate and lacked the authority to do. I even published a book integrating the 12 Steps and Jewish spirituality: *Recovery, the 12 Steps, and Jewish Spirituality: Reclaiming Hope, Courage, and Wholeness* (Jewish Lights, 2014). I looked to everything I read, every podcast I heard, every film I saw as an opportunity to learn something about how to live a meaningful and good life.

Although for years, my family life was difficult and my finances precarious, I was still able to incrementally carve out a life of meaning and fulfillment because my sense of purpose had been renewed and my Jewish identity reinvigorated again (just as on the kibbutz years before). Of course, though, this is not a fairy tale, and the path of spiritual growth is ongoing. Life is still not always easy, and both the world and I continue to change and evolve. I still make mistakes every day; I still feel resentment, fear, and discontent. I still can fall into self-pity or grandiosity, remorse, and shame. I still have my personal spiritual work to do, with much still to learn.

Today, however, I have a completely revitalized set of tools to use in times of distress and discomfort. I suppose the easiest way to sum up the difference between my darkest days of the past and today is that I have a different relationship with my own mind. I have learned tools and practices—I have a spiritual program—that "re-minds" me and helps me to release the unnecessary pain and simultaneously hold on to gratitude. The combination of releasing the unnecessary pain over things I cannot control and holding on to and reinforcing what gives me peace is what I call the "secret sauce of serenity" and of living a good life.

Intentions for This Book

Judaism is inherently broad and undefined in terms of many spiritual questions because it continuously invites us to ask, seek, and experiment with our views while simultaneously remaining faithful to one another and our practice. I believe that this uniquely Jewish invitation to ask and seek speaks to a creative spirit that animates Jewish continuity and survival. The Jewish spiritual approach is indeed to take what is true in the present, wherever one is present, and weave it into the enduring ancient collective consciousness of the Jewish canon. Jewish spirituality, therefore, is a call for courage and open spiritual boundaries, intentionally integrating all authentic seeking into its enduring narrative. For in the end, every uncovered truth is part of the continuous unfolding of God's revelation and world. This book is my humble attempt to share some of what I have learned and continue to learn in weaving my own Jewish spiritual narrative.

Thus, it is essentially a collection of explorations into spiritual growth. It is certainly an authentic and credible approach to Jewish spirituality, yet it is by no means intended to be the single authoritative view of Jewish spirituality, as it is humbly filtered through one person: me. Moreover, since I am the author, it is undoubtedly influenced by all parts of me and the fields of study that I bring and integrate into my own Jewish approach, such as psychology, philosophy, 12-Step wisdom, Hasidism, *Halakhah* (Jewish law), and American culture. Also, each chapter is largely self-contained so that readers may open it at any point and use it as a continuing resource to return to over time. Most of all, it is my hope that this book will inspire Jewish conversation and further Jewish spiritual seeking, learning, and practice.

1

A Vision of
Spiritual Growth

And the serpent said to the woman, "You are not going to die, but God knows that as soon as you eat of it, your eyes will be opened and you will be like divine beings who know good and bad." When the woman saw that the tree was good for eating and a delight to the eyes, and that the tree was desirable as a source of wisdom, she took of its fruit and ate. She also gave some to her husband, and he ate. Then the eyes of both of them were opened and they perceived that they were naked, and they sewed together fig leaves and made themselves loincloths.

—Genesis 3:4-7

"Explain me"—*darsheini.* "Explain me" is a well-known rabbinic refrain in the classical commentary on the Torah. It is used as a way for the commentator to say, "This Torah verse is confusing and needs explanation."[4] Here the commentator suggests that the Torah is complicated, mysterious, and ambiguous. And, like life itself, the Torah can be hard to understand. With both life and the Torah, much calls out, "Explain me."

The process of studying the Torah also shares the experience we find in the process of learning in life. It is a destabilizing push and pull, back and forth, with breakthroughs and setbacks. Spiritual growth means honestly and courageously engaging in this process of learning—essentially, the study of one's self.

For the Jewish tradition, the study of Torah is actually a way of studying life, as the content and subsequent questions constantly reflect back to us what we see in ourselves. Certainly, the story of the first human beings, particularly the story of Adam and Eve eating from the Tree of the Knowledge of Good and Evil, is one that draws us in, frustrates us, and finally, after deep study and self-reflection, reveals to us what it means to be human. It is surely one of the most profound and yet enigmatic sections of the Torah.

The story tells of Adam and Eve who are instructed by God that the Garden is theirs to make as their home, but are warned not to eat from one tree in the middle of the Garden: the Tree of the Knowledge of Good and Evil. Tragically, it did not take long for the couple to disregard God's directive. The serpent's temptation proved sufficient in convincing them to break this one rule their Creator had given them. The episode, from God's warning to the consequences of their infraction begs, "Explain me."

Some of the questions we might raise, include: Why is Adam told in the Garden of Eden that he should not eat from the Tree of Knowledge in the first place, and why is he told that if he does eat from it, he surely will die? Does this mean to say something about us as humans, that somehow we will die if we eat from the Tree of Knowledge? What does "consuming the fruit" from the Tree of the Knowledge of Good and Evil have to do with death? And why is it that if we eat from the Tree of Life (which is not prohibited to Adam and Eve), we presumably live forever, but eating from the Tree of Knowledge means we die?

Being Human

Before answering these questions, though, let us first consider some of our assumptions. Opening the Torah—the foundational source of Jewish spirituality and identity—it is as if we are begged to ask questions of the narrative story. And when we do, beneath their veil, we find the deeper questions: What does it mean to be in this form of ours that eventually will die—with a mind, thoughts, and feelings? And what is the relationship between body and mind, these integral parts of ourselves?

We have in our incredible brain and mind the capacity to reflect, to repeat, to rehearse, to learn, and to problem-solve. In fact, the mind is so powerful that it often seems to have a mind of its own, a will of its own, and an almost-independent perpetual momentum of its own. It is as if when we are not solving problems, we seem to be dreaming up new ones. Knowledge in its various forms, from sensory to social to "street," is the mind's fuel, and we all are filled with it. But we also have a life outside the mind, the life that is connected to other people, to family, friends, country, the land, and the world. We have an experiential life of senses, touch, and energy, as well as a life of the heart and emotions.

How does this mind, which never stops learning and self-constructing, relate to the life we actually live? How does it relate to our inner essence and being? This question—the integration of the mind into the total human experience—is a fundamental challenge and the unique human dilemma.

For a long time, people believed that knowledge was different from emotion. Many believed knowledge was transferred from some person, place, or thing into one's mind as a result of objective reality and logic, and that human reason was a tool for recognizing and transmitting objective truth. This concept of knowledge, however, has taken a shellacking of late and become harder and harder to maintain in the face of growing evidence of an integral relationship between knowledge and emotion.

For example, studies of people with brain injuries show that when those areas of the brain responsible for emotions have been damaged, the ability to solve logical problems is also impeded.[5] Of course, this should not come as a surprise, for as all of us know, whenever our emotions are unstable, we find ourselves struggling to focus and less capable of sound reasoning.

A further example of the relationship between knowledge and emotion is in the history of girls' performance in mathematics.

It used to be in the middle of the twentieth century that girls performed badly in math. Many people explained this by simply claiming that girls are innately bad at math. What we've found over the past half-century, however, is that the reason girls performed badly at math was largely because the scientific and mathematical role models the educational system had given them all were male. Because of this, taking an exam would cripple them with fear, which stifled their cognition and their capacity to use reason and logic. Thankfully, now that society has largely moved beyond such old ideas, girls today perform as well as boys in math—and are even showing signs of consistently outperforming them.[6]

As it turns out, cognition and emotion are interrelated; thinking and feeling are interrelated. Mind and heart are inextricably linked by our nervous system. Reason and feeling—knowledge and emotion—are parts of a single embracing process. Dividing human experiences into those of the mind, heart, and body, which too frequently serves to conveniently explain problems away, is truly illusory.

With this idea of the embracing interconnectedness of mind, heart, and body, let us return to the Garden of Eden and our initial questions regarding the famous "fall" of Adam and Eve: Why do they, or perhaps we all, die if we eat from the Tree of Knowledge? After all, death seems like a heavy sentence for such disobedience? Furthermore, why do we live forever if we eat from the Tree of Life?

Two Trees as One

Jewish mystics have given us an image of the two trees in the Garden that are singled out in the text, namely the Tree of the Knowledge of Good and Evil and the Tree of Life. Imagining what they must have looked like there in the Garden may deepen our understanding of the story and ourselves.[7] Instead of imagining the Tree of Knowledge and the Tree of Life as two separate trees growing in different places in the Garden, let's try imagining them as many medieval Jewish mystics did: two trees fused together.[8] In other words, let's visualize the trees as inextricably bound in this way, roots so enmeshed and trunks so entwined that they are entirely one tree. Perhaps some of us have witnessed something like this in our own yards or at a park. It is like two saplings that have grown so close together as to become one tree, and if we try to get rid of one, we will destroy the other. This is a Kabbalistic, mystical conception of the composition of the Tree of Knowledge and the Tree of Life in the Garden of Eden.

If we perceive the two as separate trees, the duality is an illusion resulting from our own perceptual limitations. The Tree of Knowledge and the Tree of Life are actually unified as one tree—which means, in effect, that when we eat from one tree, we eat from both. We may have eaten from this branch or that branch, but since they are both at their core one tree, our eating is truly from both.

In Kabbalistic literature, this understanding of the non-duality and interconnectedness of the two trees is the same view used to describe heaven. In the upper world, there are no divisions of anything. It stands in opposition to our lower world where we constantly label everything and everyone by saying, "that's good," "that's bad," "that's smart," or "that's success." Yet as we grow older and recognize that the puzzle of life grows profoundly more complex, we begin to acknowledge that such categories are truly incomplete. Spiritual wisdom, as we see with the two Trees in Eden, holds that reality is ultimately undifferentiated oneness.

And the source of evil in our lives, the slippery and sly serpent, is the force that cuts things apart and causes unnecessary divisiveness by categorizing, comparing, and inciting biting competition. What we come to learn in our process of spiritual growth is that at the highest levels—the place where God (whatever that might be) is clearly the source of all—the root of knowledge of good and evil and the root of knowledge of life itself grow as one.

Spirituality as Integration

The challenge to our spiritual growth is, therefore, integrating each of the dual and competing components of our lives that are both around us and within us. The truth is that, especially in our contemporary world, our lives are very complicated. Perhaps, when life was simpler and food and shelter were our primary concerns, less was expected of us, and our function fundamentally depended on our station in society. Centuries ago, there also may have been fewer opportunities to create divisiveness because communities had less diversity, people had less exposure to information, and fewer temptations and vices were available. Even though we in the modern, Western world should be grateful for the abundance and security that have led to longer and healthier lives, our challenges today may be as trying as ever. What may have once been the hardships of physical survival to ensure sufficient food, water, and shelter have now shifted almost entirely to adversities of the spirit and the mind.

One consequence of this has been a compartmentalization of our lives. We often consider the categories we create as if they are separate from our own being. We may speak of the problems of, "my job," "my relationship," "my family," "my school," "my health," "my time," or even "my body." What all these really are, of course, is the one me! Yet we still break these components of life, and of ourselves, into parts as if they are pieces we *have* rather than pieces that *make us*.

And besides treating these components as separate parts, we also put them into competition with one another. For instance, we might say, "My life would be fine if it just weren't for 'this thing,'" or "If I were only . . . more ambitious, less emotional, had this degree . . . then my life would be much better." Internal divisions like these bring inner turmoil and fracture, which is a set-up for continuous conflict between opposing parts of our lives, possibly leading our job to conflict with our family, our romantic relationship with our religious practice, and our use of time with our health. Such inner conflicts often lead to break-down, trauma, and crisis if they are not properly integrated.

Over the past couple of centuries of securing our individualism as citizens and political entities, we have further individualized the components of our own being. We have increasingly fragmented our being into chunks of political entities and marketing entities, each competing with one another for a limited supply of our personal energy and resources. It is no wonder that so many of us suffer from stress, anxiety, depression, sleep-deprivation, addiction, and massive caffeine consumption. We are struggling to find the energy to hold all these disparate parts of our lives together.

Sadly, many of us simply become accustomed to this numbing anxiety and accept the idea that this is simply the way of life in our time. We knowingly or unknowingly deny the possibility of spiritual integration in which the energy we need becomes available to us. We become content with being discontent, both as individuals and as a society. Rabbi Hanokh of Alexandrav touched on this notion when he taught, "The real exile for the Israelites began when they learned to endure it."

We do not need to strain to see the indifference, laziness, and greed that clog and melt away our ability to sustain vitality and life on our planet. How often do we turn on the nightly news to see example after example of the selfishly content, who sit idly by in a world saturated with injustice, violence, and terror? How many remain casually passive in a world of economic instability, poverty, and starvation? Far too many in the world are smugly satisfied, self-congratulating material successes while denying any lack of personal and spiritual progress. Of course, being content with discontent is no contentment at all.

True contentment is the result of patient and persistent spiritual seeking—studying one's life—as opposed to merely accommodating one's own temporary self-interest or shortsightedness. True contentment cannot be bought by greed or sustained by self-absorption. Such an approach leads only to more and greater desires, as do all spiritual distortions. True contentment is liberation from the false dichotomies that we unconsciously weave into our narrative of what we are supposed to be in life. It is a narrative that is shame-based and fear-based, and it whispers in the language of "either-or" and "all or nothing." Either we are successes or failures, content or miserable, good students, athletes, lovers, or bad ones; either we are too fat or too skinny, old or young, kind or callous, and so on, ad infinitum.

In this sense, Adam and Eve's mistake[9] in the Garden was an act of separation, detaching the Tree of Knowledge from the Tree of Life. Consuming the fruit was a conclusive, symbolic act of individuation and division. When they tore the fruit of knowledge away from the connected trunk, they created a split, dividing knowledge and mind from the root of the Tree of Life to which it was attached. The error of Adam and Eve lay in separating knowledge and mind from its context within all of life and life's complexity—its beauty, pain, awe, passion, sorrow, and joy. Knowledge or mind or emotion or will or any one aspect of our whole being and experience that is ripped away from the context of life becomes a source of opposition and judgment, and subsequently a fertile ground for alienation, fear, and self-pity to grow. But anything that is bound within the context and wholeness of our lives—such as our thoughts, our jobs, our families, our relationships—becomes a source of healing and a foundation for holiness to grow.

Spiritual growth is the humble process of self-integration guided by the realization and acceptance of the interconnectedness of all of life. It involves the dismantling of old ideas that breed negativity, self-doubt, and resentment, ideas caused by creating walls of false dichotomies both between each of us and others, and between the various aspects of our own being.

Spiritual growth is also an endless journey in which we are always on the way, ever moving forward, without a "there" to get to. It is a process of development of the soul, demanding rigorous honesty, daily spiritual practice, and the application of spiritual principles in everything we do, not just isolated parts or pieces. Finally, spiritual growth seeks progress by way of learning from mistakes, never expecting perfection from ourselves or anyone else.

"Turn It, and Turn It, for Everything Is in It"

Questions are essentially spiritual quests. The Jewish tradition has wisely understood that spiritual growth is an enduring, lifelong process characterized by lots and lots of questions. We are confronted with them each time the world changes as well as when we do, which is constantly. So it is that we continuously face ourselves anew. Each stage of life is a question, an opportunity for growth, an adventure of the soul in which we watch ourselves confront challenges and situations that we never thought we would. Usually, we don't know the answers or the right thing to do. Our spiritual adventure is riddled with questions.

The Jewish spiritual approach is to take these questions head-on. Thankfully, however, we never have to ask our questions alone. We have a Torah, and thousands of years of teachers from whom to learn. When we call out, "Explain me," we immediately discover that there are answers—many answers. Our spiritual work, therefore, is to live life reflectively, asking, learning, answering, and asking again. Self-reflection is the entry point for our spiritual work, but intellectual exploration is where it then turns to.

What we discover as we open the Torah is both surprising and comforting. We find accounts of neither saints nor glorified, untainted souls but of individuals with real problems. These are grounded human beings, whose families and troubles can be akin to our own—people like Abraham, who chooses to abandon his parents' ways; husbands and wives like Isaac and Rebekah, who divide their affections over their children and deal with all the ensuing pains; brothers like those who cast Joseph into the pit, who bully the cocky youngster; brothers like Simon and Levi who seek vengeance in order to protect their sister; teachers and elders such as Moses who are concerned about passing on the mantle to the next generation. And the list goes on and on, the Jewish tradition pointing us to those who have endured similar challenges and felt the same feelings we feel today.

Yet the beauty is that the process is one in which we cast our questions and doubts into the sea of thousands of years of commentary, which offers us in return timeless, sage wisdom on how to confront these problems—how to be a parent, a son, a daughter, brother, or sister, and how to be a member of a community in uncertain times.

The Torah and Jewish tradition is ultimately a reservoir or bank of emotion, thought, and spiritual wisdom in which we deposit our questions and withdraw the sustenance we need at varying times in our lives. It is an incredibly astute and wise process. At the core of the Jewish spiritual approach to living and facing life's challenges is a down-to-earth merging of heart and mind.

Finally, it is important to emphasize again that Jewish spiritual growth never ends. We do not quite get "there" because every time we complete one proverbial puzzle, a new one emerges, whether it be with our family life, our work life, or our own personal development. As Martin Buber, the great Jewish philosopher, said, "All journeys have secret destinations of which the traveler is unaware." And so we turn back to Torah, back to our questions, and back to our teachers again and again.

With this in mind, it is good to understand how the Torah itself has become the clearest embodiment of the *Etz Chayim*, the Tree of Life.[10] Somehow, the Jewish spiritual tradition has come to see that the study of Torah itself is life-sustaining and life-increasing. The more we grow in our relationship to and knowledge of Torah and the gardens of commentaries that have watered and sustained it over the millennia, the more we can appreciate its fruits. It is not always a source of comfort or joy. But neither are the other aspects of life. The Torah is a place to deposit our questions, fears, doubts, desires, and joys and then watch as they change over time, season after season, year after year, lifetime after lifetime. The early rabbinic sages understood well what it took to devote themselves to lifelong spiritual growth. Perhaps their most essential message is the one they left us about the study of Torah, this Tree of Life: *Turn it, and turn it, for everything is in it. Reflect on it and grow old and gray with it. Don't turn from it, for there is no better value than it.*[11]

2
Acknowledging Brokenness

*If you believe that breaking is possible, believe fixing is
  possible . . .
The whole world is a narrow bridge. The most
important thing is not to be afraid.*
                              —Rabbi Nachman of Bratzlav

To be human is to know breaking, to know brokenness. In fact, we are reminded of our split selves all the time. We live within the duality of the opposing ends of our experience in the world: between masculine and feminine, body and soul, heaven and earth, good and evil, and between life and death. Indeed, the Star of David itself is a symbol that indicates these opposing points—a sort of Jewish Yin and Yang—suggesting that truly harmonious living lies somewhere in the middle, where we strive for balance. To be human is to be, as Hasidic master Schneur Zalman of Liadi put it, a beinoni, or an "in-betweener."[12] What this means is to live within brokenness and splits, accepting the gray areas of life's textures and borders. As an "in-betweener" on the path of the gray textures of life, we meet brokenness, aware of what life ought to be while acknowledging the reality of what it really is.

Living amid brokenness is something that the Jewish tradition has long understood as a part of our experience. For example, the term *tikkun olam*, commonly used in many Jewish communities to mean "fixing the world," assumes that the world needs fixing.

It is based on the premise that the world was created broken, in-complete, un-whole.

But not only is the world broken; each one of us, each person, has some crack, some tear, some kind of heartbreak that needs mending and healing. Indeed, Judaism acknowledges that the fundamental experience of the human being—the innate human condition—is one of division and brokenness. Simply put, this is an imperfect world, and we are imperfect creatures.

Judaism, embodied in the canon of Torah literature, may itself be understood as a response to brokenness and heartbreak. Al-though life as a human being includes heartbreak and pain, Torah and the Jewish tradition can provide healing, as the Hasidic mas-ters teach.

> A disciple asks the rabbi: "Why does the Torah tell us to 'place these words *upon* your hearts' (Deuteronomy 11:18)? Why does it not tell us to place these holy words *in* our hearts?" The rabbi answers: "It is because as we are, our hearts are closed, and we cannot place the holy words in our hearts. So we place them on top of our hearts. And there they stay until one day, the heart breaks and the words fall in."[13]

Indeed, as a spiritual path designed to respond to such imper-fection and brokenness, Judaism offers an ingenious primary re-sponse. Rather than listing solutions for each experience, it offers us the Torah, a book filled with stories of broken and imperfect people, demonstrating that what we feel and experience has been felt and experienced before. The Torah is an affirmation of our experience.

Simply consider its most prominent figures. The first human beings, Adam and Eve, had only one rule to follow. But even in the harmonious confines of Eden, they could not adhere to it, and thus were expelled. The first child, Cain, killed his only brother. Abraham—known as the first monotheist, an emblem to all of Western religion—gives his own wife over to local kings on two different occasions, exiles his first son, Ishmael, and nearly murders his second son, Isaac. Jacob—the son after whom the Jewish people are named: Israel, which means "one who struggles with God"—is a thief and a liar, as well as a questionable father, favoring one son over the others and acquiescing to the rape of his only daughter, Dinah. Moses—the leader of the Israelites and our greatest prophet—murders a man, and must escape to the desert as a fugitive. The list of broken and imperfect biblical characters goes on. Maybe most importantly, the Jewish people as a whole—our collective national identity—is defined as having been born of brokenness, poverty, and slavery.

Clearly, these descriptions of biblical heroes omit much that is to be admired about them. Highlighting less-than-virtuous aspects of their lives does not diminish their greatness (as it should not for anyone). The Torah simply wants to present our ancestors as actual human beings, and only by including their imperfections and mistakes can it truly validate their humanity. By doing this, it wisely teaches us that imperfection is not a curse but a part of life, and that success is measured by how we persist toward goodness despite our imperfections. If the Torah merely offered saints for us to emulate, it would be a sterile and irrelevant document, because we would all hopelessly and shamefully fall short. The Torah is a teaching for *us*, for human beings in this real world, not for gods in a galaxy far away. By acknowledging the failures and errors of our ancestors, it reflects back to us what we all need to know: Everybody fails, everybody errs, and everybody falls— *and* that does not need to be the whole of our story nor its end.

Even with the Torah's explicit acknowledgment of human brokenness, however, many of us still strive for perfection and struggle to cope with the inherent dilemma of living as "in-betweeners." We are sensitive to life's brokenness, such as injustice and violence, and so we seek absolute and perfect solutions. No one wants to dwell in the tension and discomfort of life's complex and uncertain reality. We seek control.

The reality of our human experience is multidimensional, with thoughts, feelings, and physiology all bound together as one. Comprehending it demands time and reflection. We experience sorrow and joy, bitterness and compassion, gratitude and loss all at once. The feelings live within us simultaneously and are triggered in experiential associations all at once.

The loss of a loved one, for example, may raise feelings of sadness but also of both resentment for an action in the past and gratitude for something else. In such a complicated experience, we are tempted to compartmentalize or deny parts of it. That is where our spiritual growth most needs work. If in a case like this, we do not attend to both the life-affirming and the pain, we may be left with only uncertainty and confusion. To have resentment left bound together with sadness and gratitude can be overwhelmingly distressing and unnerving.

A common response, unfortunately, is to "stuff" or repress those feelings in an attempt to control them. Whether we are conscious of it at first or not, denying the resentment and sadness (and sometimes even the gratitude) forces us into a process of self-control that requires a tremendous amount of energy and self-consciousness. It is an untenable long-term strategy, denying the psyche the freedom it needs to function and grow. Though they may build unnoticed over time, self-centered control and expression of unacknowledged brokenness are often the tragic outcome.

Temptations of Control

Today, all sorts of societal temptations purporting to help us control our human experience and conquer distress are in reality only the marketing strategies of companies seeking to sell us their wares and snake-oil salves. And yet we buy them. We hope they will let us control and solve our internal problems through material goods that sate us. But such goods, though they may ease discomfort at times, are only partial and temporary. They lead us to continue on that route, compelled to buy the next "best" thing in order to maintain the sense of progress and reward—all the while avoiding the essential inner dilemma.

We may also try to control our internal life through the external comfort that can be found in romantic relationships. But however beautiful and sacred a part of life they may be, they cannot "solve" our internal angst. Though we may attach to someone in an attempt to fix or remove what is within us, no amount of another person's presence, intelligence, beauty, money, or touch will satisfy us.

Many people who struggle being alone with themselves move from one relationship to another searching for someone who can distract or soothe them. Many others remain far too long in unhealthy, codependent relationships, choosing dysfunction over the anxiety and discomfort of facing themselves alone. We cling in such cases to the false idea that either something outside ourselves will save us from despair or that we are not worthy of anything better.

Deep within, we know that healthy relationships are ones in which each person identifies, admits, and accepts his or her own imperfections. Healthy relationships involve vulnerability and are motivated by acceptance and forgiveness, leading to greater interdependence rather than codependence; i.e., a relationship of mutual responsibility and collaboration toward each other's greater interests and selves. Ultimately, healthy romantic relationships lift both partners to their best selves, proving that the true experience of love is ascendance and elevation rather than something we "fall" into.

In addition, many of us look for intellectual or symbolic external security to deal with our inner tensions. Degrees from distinguished universities, important jobs with prestigious companies, and big corner offices give many of us a sense of accomplishment—but yet they spare no one from the problems of living, often giving instead only a yearning for more of what cannot meet our true needs. The perfect resume is no defense against heartbreak or emotional emptiness. At our deepest core, we know that the human experience is riddled with a vulnerability from which no title, power, or prestige can protect or relieve us.

Alcohol and drug abuse are certainly dramatic examples of behavior that seeks to control our internal suffering with external solutions. Mind-altering substances seem to give us this control by distracting us or numbing our emotional response to imperfection, uncertainty, and vulnerability. But there also are other obsessive ways people try to control their internal lives, including workaholism, rampant caffeine consumption, overeating, prescription drug abuse, diet pill abuse, gambling, internet pornography, shopaholism, hoarding, video game addiction, smart phone and social media compulsion, sex addiction, co-dependency, bullying, anorexia, bulimia, and self-mutilation. Each of these behaviors results from an external approach to controlling our internal selves.

While indulging in our compulsive and addictive behaviors, we may feel in control of our lives, minds, and feelings, but this, of course, is a delusion. It must collapse in order for us to live healthy, whole, and integrated lives, accepting that we are never truly in total control. After all, we do not exist alone in the world. We cannot control how we are connected to the rest of it and continuously influenced by other people, whether we like it or not. Ultimately, it is how we understand and relate to the world, to others, and to God that provides our sense of wellbeing.

Either gradually or suddenly, the subtle and persistent delusion that we are isolated entities in the world must crash, and when it does, we are often left with the consequences of our stubborn, self-absorbed worldview. We cannot avoid the human struggle of existing as an "in-betweener," without the illusion of control. Once we honestly confront our raw and mysterious existence, we are faced with a choice: Will we live in hope, courage, and joy, contributing to the blessings and lives around us, or will we live in hopelessness, fear, and despair, injecting more anguish and suffering into the world? Will we choose life and blessing or death and curse?

The essence of spiritual growth is to accept the fact of what it means to be an "in-betweener." We must acknowledge that to be human is to know the brokenness both of the world and within ourselves. This acceptance awakens us to the fact that the divisions of that brokenness are what constitute the whole of our reality and experience. Each piece, although divided and perhaps even contradictory (e.g., good and evil, joy and sorrow), represents a perspective of truth. Once we accept this, we can begin to grow by integrating these pieces into a more-unified and all-embracing truth.

Accepting what it means to be an "in-betweener" also means surrendering to the fact that we are not in ultimate control of our lives. Our spiritual growth depends on accepting life on its own terms and abandoning our attempts to play God by turning to what we appear to control. We must acknowledge that all we know for sure is that we live—often in conditions that are unfavorable, to say the least—and that we die. Our birth into a world that we did not create, and may not even condone, and the fact that we are destined to experience pain while we are in it and to die at the end are not of our own will.[14] Only in sincerely accepting this reality, truly and affirmatively choosing this life, can we mindfully and consciously live it.

Brokenness as a Spiritual Premise

Human brokenness is not new. It is the quintessential existential human dilemma, and lies at the foundation of many spiritual traditions. From them in response comes the claim that amid our powerlessness, there is a power greater than ourselves—such as a God, or gods, or a truth at the core of the universe—that is responsible for the way of the world. Our drive to resist this Power or God by asserting our own power and clinging to the immediate fulfillment of our desires is futile and vain. If we are wise, rather than resisting this, we accept it, gaining power by aligning our own will with God's.[15]

Spiritual traditions use several terms to describe our efforts to be in control. Essentially, the experience is characterized by an emotional discomfort, resulting in outward reaching toward something that will comfort us. When we've fixed our sights on that object or behavior, we think about it obsessively until an almost-physiological response occurs. It is as if possessing it or acting on it is the only way we will be satisfied. Spiritual sages and literature often refer to this as desire or attachment; others call it lust, craving, clinging, or greed. Fundamentally, they are all referring to this same experience.

We recognize such a spiritual description in the Hindu Upanishads:

> When all desires that cling to the heart are
> surrendered, then a mortal becomes immortal . . . .
> A man whose mind wanders among desires, and is
> longing for objects of desire, goes again to life and
> death according to his desires. But he who possesses
> the end of all longing, and whose self has found
> fulfillment, even in this life his desires will fade away.[16]

We recognize it as clinging, craving, and desire (also often translated as attachment) in the Four Noble Truths of Buddhism, summarized as follows:

• Suffering is a fact of life. In brief, clinging to the ways in which a person experiences the world is suffering;

• Suffering is caused by craving to become something that one is not, and by clinging to delight and desires;

• Liberation from suffering and the reinstitution of human freedom can happen only through release from that craving and an end to our clinging to desires; and

• Human effort toward release from craving and clinging to desires must involve all aspects of one's life in a deeply spiritual way.[17]

We recognize this also in the Christian Bible as desirous "love":

Do not love the world or the things in the world. If anyone loves the world, the love of the Father is not in him. For all that is in the world—the desires of the flesh and the desires of the eyes and pride in possessions—is not from the Father but is from the world. And the world is passing away along with its desires, but whoever does the will of God abides forever.[18]

And we recognize it in the Hebrew Bible:

I withheld from my eyes nothing that they desired, and refused my heart no pleasure . . . and oh, it was all futile and pursuit of wind; there was no real value under the sun![19]

In each example, we see that the pursuit of control through desire and clinging is not be squelched but rather redirected to a greater purpose, or to God. We must accept that the desire to ease discomfort exists but also that we are best served by directing this same energy toward a greater good which unites rather than further divides us.

In other words, the great spiritual traditions of the world share the fundamental spiritual assertion that when we replace our desire for connection with the Divine—whether defined as a transcendent sense of self, a collective consciousness, or God— we distort and diminish our experience. Christian existentialist Paul Tillich and Jewish theologian Abraham Joshua Heschel both defined God as that which is our "ultimate" in our life, and the religious traditions continuously warn that at any given moment, we are susceptible to making something that is not the true God into our ultimate concern.[20]

In this light, it is fitting that the central statement of the Jewish faith—the *Shema*—which is traditionally recited each morning and night, is one of directing all of one's faculties toward God, understood to be the one unifying source of all blessing:

> Hear o Israel, the Lord our God, the Lord is one.
> You shall love the Lord your God with all your heart
> and all your soul and all your might.[21]

The Jewish tradition is very sensitive to the fact that controlling and obsessive behaviors can usurp our concern for what is actually sacred and Divine. Potentially, however, all sorts of daily interactions can become our ultimate concern if we allow them to, such as the dramas of our relationships, buying the right brand of clothing, or posting a status update on a social media site. This distortion of attention from what is right and of ultimate value can subtly and silently occupy one's entire life if left untended. These behaviors represent a resistance to accepting the divisions in our experience as parts of the one whole; they are a way of directing our energies to the absolute ends of our brokenness, as we seek a greater sense of control. Different faiths recognize this in different ways; in Judaism, the deepest and most significant rendering for it is idolatry.

Untended Brokenness Leads to Idolatry

For centuries, rabbis and Jewish sages have known that idolatry is not merely about bowing down to graven images of stone and wood. In his *Guide for the Perplexed*, the twelfth-century scholar Maimonides presented a clear understanding of idolatry as a metaphor for "respecting an image of thing that is an intermediary between ourselves and God."[22] And that "image of thing" could take all sorts of material or behavioral forms. Modern versions of these "idols," rabbis have suggested, include our fame, our wealth,[23] our pride.

Regarding pride, which is undoubtedly the emotional root associated with fame and wealth, Shneur Zalman of Liadi states:

> Pride is truly equivalent to idolatry. For the main
> root principle of idolatry consists in man's

acknowledgement of something existing in its own right apart and separate from God's holiness.[24]

The essential point here is that idolatry is the sin of acting as if something is divine that is not divine. The key Jewish assumption that makes idolatry a sin is that somewhere within our core spiritual composition, we know the difference between what is divine and what is not. In rabbinic language, we might say that each of us is made in the image of God (*b'tzelem Elohim*) and that we—consciously or unconsciously—are bound to the abiding truth of God. Therefore, anytime we attach to or use an object, idea, or behavior to mediate our value in the world, we are denying the truth of God to which we are inherently bound. We are denying the truth about ourselves, and belittling the divine value of our own lives and our sacred purpose in the world.

One of the most lucid representations of the controlling, idolatrous disposition in Jewish literature comes from the *Sefat Emet*, by Yehudah Aryeh Leib Alter of Ger (who was known by the name of that same Hasidic masterpiece). In it, we find a striking comment on a well-known passage in the Book of Exodus. When Moses, in Chapter 6, goes before Pharaoh and asks that the Israelite slaves be freed, Pharaoh famously increases their burden, driving Moses to return to God in despair, asking why God allows this suffering to happen. God replies by instructing Moses to tell the Israelites that God will save and redeem them. The episode concludes, though, with a harrowing line:

> But when Moses told this to the Israelites, *they would not listen to Moses, their spirits were crushed by cruel bondage* (Exodus 6:9).

This critical verse raises the questions: Why wouldn't the Israelites listen? What does it mean that "their spirits were crushed"? Even though none of us were slaves in Egypt, we can imagine the harsh cruelty they experienced. We can also imagine that the suffering was so great and continued for so long that it was simply impossible to believe Moses's promise of liberation; all they had known was slavery. Those answers may be true, but the *Sefat Emet* takes it one step further:

> When it says that *they would not listen to Moses* (Exodus 6:9), the Midrash says that it was hard for them to abandon their idolatry . . . . Listening requires being empty of everything. *Hear, O daughter, and see, give ear; forget your people and your father's house* (Psalms 45:11). This is the essence of exile today as well: our inability to empty ourselves, to forget this world's vanities so that we empty the heart to hear God's word without any distracting thought. This is the meaning of the verse: *Do not turn after your hearts [or after your eyes]* (Numbers 15:39). And it was because *no man would cast away the abominations of his eyes* (Ezekiel 20:8) that they walked about amid "the idols of Egypt." Had they been ready to hear God's word, they would have been redeemed immediately.[25]

The *Sefat Emet* suggests that the Israelites could not listen to Moses because they were in a deep state of spiritual hopelessness caused by idolatry. They were so immersed in the life of slavery, knowing only Pharaoh's power and dominance over their lives, that they believed only in Pharaoh's power and not God's. The redemptive promise of God was simply alien. They may have been able intellectually to accommodate a faith in God, as one commentator suggests,[26] but the fact was that their "hearts and eyes"— what they felt and experienced—could not accept that God's redemptive love was truly possible.

The experience of the Israelites was a feeling of powerless-ness, not in the sense of inability to accept a true divine power but rather a sense of hopelessness. Genuine spiritual powerlessness is surrender to the infinite possibility of the divine. What we see here is powerlessness without surrender—actually a clinging to the certainty of hopelessness, and any clinging to a certainty is a form of emotional control and personal pride. This is the expression of clinging to absolutes, and the *Sefat Emet* is crystal clear in his analysis that it is the same spiritual exile that was experienced in his time and which we certainly see today.

Interestingly, what the *Sefat Emet* offers, from Psalms 45:11, is that the spiritual path to opening ourselves to "hearing" the truth of God's infinite possibility is forgetting what we know from the past—"to forget your people and your father's house." In other words, we must empty ourselves of the world's ideas and vanities—the idols we have clung to—which have constituted our spiritual system of belief until now, so as to be open anew and able to "listen" to the divine call of redemption's possibility.

Acceptance and Action

The opposing poles of the world and our human nature have been identified and included in the Jewish tradition for millennia. The problems they cause are as old as time, and so are the solutions. The starting point begins with acknowledging these inner divisions. One medieval rabbinic commentator may have expressed our inherent nature best when he wrote:

> It is because man is half-angel and half-brute that his inner life witnesses such bitter war between such unlike natures. The brute in him clamors for sensual joy and things in which there is only vanity; but the angel resists and strives to make him know that meat, drink, and sleep are but means whereby the body may be made ready for the study of truths and the doing of the will of God. Not until the very hour

of death can it be certain or known to what measure
the victory has been won.[27]

This incredible statement articulates what *is* rather than what
should be. It is an authentic expression of acceptance—true acceptance and acknowledgment of what is real. From there, we
can begin to heal the tragic gap that is causing our internal dis-
unity. Acceptance is, after all, the primary goal of spiritual practice, giving us the clarity to navigate the world as we wish.
Without it, we are inclined toward resentment and control, clinging to something less than sacred—an idol—the exact opposite
of where every spiritual tradition has pointed.

Perhaps the most concise representation of this idea—
namely, choosing acceptance over clinging to temporary
"idols"—is what is commonly known as the "Serenity Prayer,"
from Reinhold Niebuhr:

> God, grant me the serenity to accept the things
> I cannot change; the courage to change the things
> I can; and the wisdom to know the difference.

Encapsulated in this brief prayer are the three central elements
of spiritual growth. First is acceptance. This acceptance is not resignation, acquiescence, or giving up. It is an internal shift toward
the freedom to no longer fight the stream of life by trying to control it but rather to surrender to its power and wonder, so that
we can more easily see where we need to steer. Acceptance is the
humble posture in which we place ourselves within the natural
stream of the reality of life.

Second is courage, which is the most important quality for living a whole, integrated, and happy life. It is the ability to acknowledge where we are afraid and uncertain, and then, despite that
fear and anxiety, take the needed steps toward being good and
doing what is right. Courage is the necessary predecessor to faith.

Finally, wisdom is the essential outcome of true acceptance. It flows from the acceptance of our brokenness, our imperfections, our heartbreak, our powerlessness, and the fact that we are "in-betweeners." Once we accept our imperfections, we can cease being self-conscious and self-centered, and can direct our attention wholly toward the world and the people in it, recognizing what actually is. Our ability to make decisions toward what is right and good becomes more attuned and accurate. So it is that from acceptance, we gain the wisdom to take right action.

Spiritual growth, therefore, is the process by which we courageously and mindfully work toward greater self-acceptance, resisting our compulsion to control either the world around us or our own inner world. Spiritual growth is unlocking our unifying wisdom to marry the opposing ends of our experiences in order to live an integrated life of wholeness. Spiritual growth is also an ongoing process of hearing anew, gaining insights through study and reflection, and developing practices that help us navigate the complexity of human experience. Finally, spiritual growth is our means to illuminate and nurture an intimate relationship with the Divine, Greater Power, or God.

3
Awakening to
Our Story

*What good is the understanding of a text if one does not
thereby attain a better understanding of oneself?*
— Rabbi Menachem Mendel of Kotzk

Our days in this world are wrapped in stories. From morning
until night, we are saturated with them. Our media and
culture are constantly telling stories in the news, TV, movies, literature, and the arts. Our country, our families, and each of us
tells a story. When we simply tell someone about our day, we are
telling a story, one of the many stories that determine the meaning of our lives and tell us who we are.

In Jewish mystical literature, storytelling is one of the pillars
of the creation of the universe, as the basis of communication.[28]
It is therefore no wonder that a spiritual tradition such as Judaism
is founded on a sacred story, namely the Torah. Of course, the
Torah is only the start of storytelling for Judaism. Classical rabbinic literature is characterized by its stories and parables. Mystical and Hasidic literature leans on stories as the primary means
of spiritual expression and teaching. The first century Aramaic
scholar Onkelos regarded the essential nature of the human being
as a "soul that speaks,"[29] and it is primarily stories that we speak.

The value of these stories is that they give the spiritual values
our lives are based on a context and relevance that is essential if
we are to understand the depth and complexity of the spiritual
issues at stake and how to apply them in our lives. Stories seem

to have an almost-magical ability to convey the breadth and depth of human experience more successfully than any other means of communication. As anthropologist and linguist Gregory Bateson tells us:

> A man wanted to know about mind, not in nature but in his private large computer. He asked it, "Do you compute that you will ever think like a human being?" The machine then set to work analyzing its computational habits. Finally, the machine printed its answer on a piece of paper, as such machines do. The man ran to get the answer and found, neatly typed, the words: THAT REMINDS ME OF A STORY.[30]

Bateson's anecdote points to what makes us distinctly human by comparing how we as mortal beings think with how a computer "thinks." With a comic twist, it punctuates the fact that, at our spiritual core, we are storytellers. The point here, however, is not only that we tell stories but also that the reason they penetrate so deeply is that we think in stories. Our minds are story warehouses. As opposed to computers, which answer problems by retrieving numerical data and adhering to preprogrammed algorithms, we can respond by drawing on morals and principles embedded in the context of stories we have learned or experienced. Thus, the Torah and other sacred literature naturally come to us in the form of stories, the most effective medium for relating what it means to be human.

Throughout time, stories have given us ways to deal with deep and wide spiritual questions. Who are we? Why are we here? How should we live? Only stories can handle these questions, because only stories can convey the subtleties of life that touch on the whole human complex of our cognitive, emotional, and spiritual dimensions. Physics, chemistry, and biology may be able to describe the make-up of the universe, but they cannot convey the entirety of our experience because they neglect the dimension of affect. The truth of our experience must not only capture the exacting data of life but also recognize the emotion, the slow-turning movement of spirit, and the psychological momentum that distinguish our humanity. Rabbi Nachman of Bratzlav, a master storyteller, made this point well:

> Man is incapable of a sudden confrontation with his Creator. The overwhelming experience of such awareness is just too awesome. Truth, the stark Truth, must be camouflaged. Only then can the soul gradually absorb it.
>
> God, so to speak, camouflaged Himself in stories. These are the stories of the Creation and of Adam and Eve; the stories of the Flood and of the Patriarchs; the stories of Jewish exile and redemption. God is hidden in all the stories of human history, and in the as-yet-untold stories of each and every human being—his trials, his tribulations, and his salvation . . . .
>
> As we relate the details of these stories, we must relate to them. Be aroused by them. See the Hand of God in the stories of our own lives.[31]

It is noteworthy that Rabbi Nachman also said that some stories are to put our children to sleep and others are to wake us up. Spiritual growth hinges on our ability to wake up, and stories can help make this happen if we open our minds, hearts, and souls to hear them. If a story is told that we merely judge, criticize, and passively observe at a distance, saying to ourselves that it applies "to them, not me," we miss out on the possibility of weaving more meaning, more possibility, more hope, and more courage into our personal stories. When we meet the storytellers, whether on the page or in person, elevating our minds and hearts to their words, putting ourselves in their places[32] and absorbing their energy can awaken us to the mutual spiritual experiences that reveal both truths about our life and, as Rabbi Nachman put it, "the Hand of God."

The Misfortune of Stories in Our Time

In the past several decades, especially with the massive onset of technology, our lives seem to have speeded up. The friends we used to call on our phones one digit at a time we now speed-dial without considering a single number. Once we would buy and read books; now we download them and speed-read with the click of button. There is even "speed yoga," marketed as instant spiritual relief for the upwardly mobile, busy professional seeking to burn more calories faster.[33]

Technology and the internet have certainly given us rapid access to all sorts of lifestyle accommodations, from Amazon to Lyft. Although this technology is supposed to make life easier and help us manage our time more effectively, for many people, the opposite is true. Technology has actually made our lives more complicated with the barrage of information and messaging constantly being blasted at us. So-called time-saving devices have sucked up most of our time and given us more to do—not less. Just look at what's involved in merely keeping up with email, texts, passwords, and syncing devices?

Ernest Kurtz and Katherine Ketchum in their masterpiece, *The Spirituality of Imperfection*, write of the transcendent impact on our lives of slowing down to genuinely communicate and connect with one another, rather than speeding up. They make the case for the power of taking the time to tell and listen to stories, so they can help us to live humanly. Kurtz and Ketchum lament that the patient practice of storytelling has fallen by the wayside in an era when instant gratification doesn't seem fast enough. Instant response and instant information have only given us a craving for more expediency, which masks our clinging to a sense of control over our fast-moving and complicated lives. In turn, our ability to willingly sit and attend to the basic questions of meaning and spirituality has seriously diminished.

Kurtz and Ketchum echo the point of the great scholar of mythology Joseph Campbell when he spoke of modernity's loss of touch with the power of stories:

> One of our problems today is that we are not well acquainted with the literature of the spirit. We're interested in the news of the day and the problems of the hour . . . .
>
> Greek and Latin and biblical literature used to be a part of everyone's education. Now, when these were dropped, a whole tradition of Occidental mythological information was lost. It used to be that these stories were in the minds of people. When the story is in your mind, then you see its relevance to something happening in your own life. It gives you perspective on what's happening to you . . . These bits of information from ancient times, which have to do with the themes that have supported human life, built civilizations, and informed religions over millennia, have to do with deep inner problems, inner mysteries, inner thresholds of passage, and if you don't know what the guide-signs are along the way, you have to work it out yourself. But once this subject catches you, there is such a feeling, from one or another of these traditions, of information of a deep, rich, life-vivifying sort that you don't want to give it up.[34]

One of today's greatest complaints is that we do not have time. And in this apparent loss of time, we also lose our sense of seeking. With no time to spare, we deny our genuine ambivalence and uncertainty about life—we have no time for it—and reach instead for the quick answers of the internet and Wikipedia. Such quick fixes, however, do not heal the deep angst of being in the mystery of life. Quick fixes do not honor the real pain of living with loss, loneliness, and feelings of shame. As Campbell indicated, without the language of spirit, without the power of stories, we lose the grounding foundation with which humanity has managed its daily lives. Stories frame the polarities of life's experience of good and evil, heaven and earth, piety and temptation in a singularity that lets us engage in the totality of reality. They may not change the facts we encounter on the ground, but they can change our experience of those facts by the ways in which they raise our minds and hearts in response to them.

The Gift of the Rabbis

It is fair to say that many stories we tell are not factually, historically, or empirically true. There is even good evidence that many of the central stories of the Torah itself are unlikely to be historically or scientifically factual. It is hard to believe, for example, that there was a donkey that spoke, as is told in the Book of Numbers.[35] It is hard to fathom the empirical reality of a talking snake in the Garden of Eden, Lot's wife turning into a pillar of salt, the Ten Plagues, the splitting of seas, and manna raining from heaven. But we miss the mythical power and, frankly, the point of these stories if we only focus on their empirical facts. Moreover, when we look into stories for the historical facts they contain, our minds tend to narrow into a judgmental and analytical posture, while the potential truth that the story reveals often is lost on us. This modern critical, academic posture is a major reason our ancient stories have been discounted as reliable sources of truth and wisdom.

Ancient stories and the Torah were not written to be read through the lens of the scientific method. They are poetry—epic poetry—and should be understood as such. As poetry, they contain infinite levels of understanding and interpretation. We are not supposed to take the stories of the Torah literally. Figurative, as opposed to literal, interpretation is precisely the basis of Rabbinic Judaism, which defines what we recognize as the Jewish tradition today.

The purpose of these stories when viewed this way is not to change reality as we understand it. They are not there to convince us that the laws of nature might take some time off, and that donkeys might actually talk or that seas might split. The purpose of stories is to change us. They change the state of our minds and thus the reality of our experience. And, likewise, the state of our minds is determined by the stories we tell—both to others and, perhaps more importantly, to ourselves. If we tell hopeful stories, it is more likely we will be hopeful; if we tell depressing stories, it is more likely we will be depressed. If we tell stories of miracles, we are more likely to be open to the miracles of every day.

Now, let us indulge in a story:

An old and long-standing monastery had recently fallen on hard times. A sort of darkness had come over the monks there, which did not help attract other monks to either join or remain in the order. The monastery was dying.

The head abbot did not know what to do. "How can we continue the order with only a handful of monks remaining?" he thought. As he was praying on the darkening state of his monastery, the abbot remembered a rabbi who lived in a village close by. The rabbi was a quiet man, but maybe, the abbot thought, he would have some advice, some wisdom to offer in this trying time.

The rabbi welcomed the abbot into his humble house and listened intently to the explanation of how the spirit of hope and faith seemed to have been drained out of his monastery, and the inability to attract new members that followed.

"I do know something about that," said the rabbi, hinting at his own synagogue's problems.

"Well," exclaimed the abbot desperately, "is there any advice you might have that you can offer to help me save my dying order?"

"I'm sorry," said the rabbi. "I'm afraid I really don't know what to tell you. I don't know much about such matters." Then the rabbi paused and slowly stroked his beard.

"I do know one thing, though, about your order," the rabbi said, staring into the abbot's eyes. "The one thing I know is that among those in your order is the messiah."

The abbot was astonished and hurried back with this unexpected and yet promising news. He gathered the remaining monks and shared what the rabbi had told him: "Among our order, one of us is the messiah."

The monks were shocked. They looked at each other, wondering if it could be true, and if so, who it could possibly be. Some thought it must be the Father Abbot himself. Others thought it could be Brother Thomas because of his kindness. Some thought it had to be Brother Phillip because of his devotion to his practices. But no one really knew for sure.

Over the next days and weeks, the feeling around the monastery began to change. The monks started walking the halls with a renewed sense of dignity and respect. They were kinder and more generous with one another. After all, the very person they were with might be the messiah! Or perhaps, each one felt, he himself was the messiah, and should behave in a manner becoming of the messiah.

Soon enough, word began to spread to the surrounding villages that the messiah was among the monks at the nearby monastery. Pilgrims and tourists began to visit. The visitors would converse with the monks, pray in the monastery's gardens, and bring gifts. Everyone who visited returned home with a report about the extraordinary aura of respect and serenity permeating the atmosphere of the monastery.

It wasn't long before younger monks began to join the order, and by the next year, the once-struggling monastery had become a thriving community of hope, courage, and peace.[36]

The resonance and truth of this touching story is not in its facts or premises. The story's truth is actually about the power stories have to change us. Nothing about the monastery or the order is really changed by what the rabbi told the abbot. It was simply a story. And with the telling of that story, everything changes.

Everything changes because the minds of the order's monks are changed, even if they are not sure whether the story is true. The mere possibility of its truth is enough to change their minds, which changes their behavior, which then eventually changes the facts on the ground. The story of the rabbi and the abbot is a story of mind, feeling, and spirit—and of the resounding power stories have in ways unlike any other form of expression.

Owning Our Story

Awakening to the meaning and power of stories is a vital aspect of spiritual growth. This may seem simple, yet in the mundane, rapid routine of daily life, it is easy to become distracted from the narrative that pervades each of our experiences. To awaken to stories calls for slowing down and paying attention, and for the humble willingness to listen to what we may have to learn.

Of all of the stories we encounter during our day, spiritual growth demands that we pay most attention to our own story. Again, this may seem simple. But as we listen to our minds and awaken to the story we tell ourselves, many people find that our stories speak of negativity, of self-doubt, resentment, and despair. We tell ourselves we do not deserve happiness, prosperity, and other things in our lives because of our shame about events in the past. We find our stories blaming others for what is happening to us. We see them creating conditions such as, "Once I have such and such degree, job, salary, or relationship, then I'll be happy," or "If only I had this, or if that person would just be better to me, I would be fine." Elements like these that we write into our stories prevent us from awakening to our true power and growing into our potential. But what we must remember is that we have been given the freedom to write our stories as we choose.

To do this, to choose the stories we write for ourselves, we must first own the story we have. This is the process of recognizing that life is an adventurous journey. We will take some wrong turns; we will hit some dead ends; we will face injustices and heartbreak. We will fall. But the moment we are living now is a testament to our ability to survive. The circumstances that led to this point—the actions of others, the mistakes we made ourselves—do not have to be the defining chapters of our story.

Owning our story means listening to it courageously and honestly, and taking responsibility for it. It means discarding the lies we've told ourselves—our victimhood or our arrogant superiority—and giving ourselves permission to step forward into the adventure that is beckoning to us at every moment. Yes, we may have suffered unjustly in the past, and yes, we may have every right to be angry. But at this point today, we are okay, and we can choose whether to perpetuate our old cycle of spiritual cause and effect or stop it in its tracks. We can be present, here and now, neither victim of the past nor anxiously straining to predict the future. It is in this experience of the present that the power of myth and miracle, the beauty of poetry and music, begin to be written into our narrative. Joseph Campbell again, when discussing the inward journey of our own story, called it "following your bliss":

> It is miraculous. I even have a superstition that has grown on me . . . namely, that if you do follow your bliss, you put yourself on a kind of track that has been there all the while, waiting for you, and the life that you ought to be living is the one you are living. When you can see that, you begin to meet people who are in your field of bliss, and they open doors to you. I say, follow your bliss and don't be afraid, and doors will open where you didn't know they were going to be.[37]

"Bliss," as Campbell describes it, is the outcome of sincere spiritual growth through the heroic quest of awakening to, owning, and then courageously writing the epic adventure of our lives.

4

Facing Our Counterpart

Man is afraid of things that cannot harm him, and he knows it; and he craves things that cannot help him, and he knows it. But actually, it is something within man he is afraid of, and it is something with man that he craves.[38]

—Hasidic teaching

Everything that God created is good. This is not a statement of some stargazing idealist. This is the Torah. In the first chapter of Genesis, throughout the days of creation, God looks and "saw that it was good."[39] The chapter goes on to conclude by saying, "And God saw all that He had made, and found it very good." Because we have read ahead, however, we know that not everything in God's creation was and is good, certainly not very good! One needs to read only a few more chapters in the Torah to discover murder, corruption, violence, lawlessness, and catastrophe.

The Torah itself is not the only account that tells of the creation of the world as "all good." The Kabbalists, or Jewish mystics, offer a blueprint of the cosmos called the *Sefirot*. There are ten *Sefirot*, which can be understood as divine emanations or dimensions, referring to the spiritual elements that make up both the world as a whole and each one of our own souls. Among the *Sefirot* are elements such as Wisdom, Understanding, Lovingkindness, Judgment, Harmony, Victory, Splendor, all of which are good or positive qualities. None among them is inherently evil or bad.

Considering both the Torah and the Kabbalistic conceptions of the creation of the world, we may wonder how to account for the bad or evil that exists. If evil is not a part of creation itself, how does it come to be manifest in the world? Does it have a purpose? How do we get rid of it? (There is tragic irony, of course, in the fact that the Jewish people, whose basic theology does not recognize evil as an inherent part of the world, have historically been the victims of so much evil.)

The process of spiritual growth involves understanding and accepting our human experience, including what we often deem bad or evil. Sickness, suffering, and death can be caused by nature, by other people, or even by our own doing. Whether this happens intentionally or unintentionally, we are often left wondering why. Why did this happen? Why is it a part of my experience? Why can't everything I encounter be "very good," as God created?

Beyond the Jewish tradition's acknowledgement of the presence of pain in life, and of evil in the world, there is a stream of Jewish spiritual thought that believes pain and evil may be opportunities for growth. While the idea is certainly not comforting to those in the throes of pain and loss, it nonetheless offers the understanding that everything we experience is to help us grow and learn. If we can understand each experience as temporary, rather than something that characterizes the soul's entire journey, we may be able to open ourselves to experiencing particular pain and suffering at varying levels. We can see sometimes that events which were temporarily painful brought about growth and a deepening of heart that led to greater strength. Looking across the entire spectrum of time, we may find that what was confusion, discomfort, or even evil turned out to be a source of understanding, comfort, and even goodness. From this expansive spiritual perspective, what is bad may not actually be bad.

Of course, national and international tragedies and acts of mass violence sometimes are so horrific we cannot see any good that would come from them. In the realm of personal experiences, the individual journey of each one of our spirits, we must look upon the pain and find in it opportunities for acceptance, courage, and forgiveness, so that we can learn and progress in our growth.

Integrating Essential Pain

Life will inevitably bring heartbreak, pain, and what we experience as evil. This is one of its essential features, and none of us is spared. We must admit, however, that we do not need to suffer unnecessarily because of our own limited and imperfect understanding and perspective. Far too frequently, what we suffer is self-imposed, and what begins as an essential life pain, such as heartbreak, loss, or injury, turns into lingering bouts of unnecessary suffering. Far too often, we stand in the way of our own relief from pain. As the Hasidic teaching says:

> Man himself is the source of all his troubles,
> for the light of God pours over him eternally. But
> through his all-too-bodily existence, man comes to
> cast a shadow, so that the light cannot reach him.[40]

Spiritual growth is a process of confronting the essential pains of life as teachers, as opportunities for growth, not as necessary evils. But what we can learn from them depends on our ability to humbly confront ourselves and to distinguish the pain that helps us do this from our own inner conflict and division. We must distinguish between what is real and what are, in fact, our own preexisting issues and baggage. Although it is disturbing to be rear-ended by a car whose driver was not paying attention, if we become preoccupied with an incident like this or blow it out of proportion, such as by threatening retribution and violence, what happened becomes not about being rear-ended but rather a manifestation of something within us that has not been resolved. This is self-imposed, unnecessary suffering.

Let us be clear: Distinguishing between real pain and our own emotional and psychological baggage is no small matter; it's hard spiritual work. These unresolved inner divisions and their baggage usually go back a long way, twisting through our lives for decades. Once triggered, they can be very powerful. To grow, we must raise them up to the surface, face them, accept them, and integrate them into our worldview. We might say our work is to accept that each of us has a "counterpart" within ourselves that works either against us or for us. It can be a source of pain and inner turmoil or of learning and growth—it's our choice.

Because we all share a universal spiritual makeup, we share this counterpart on the most basic levels. The first is on the existential level, the divided part of the self that has not accepted life lived in this world and in this form as humans. This represents a personal and spiritual division about existence itself.

The second level is the egoic counterpart, the nature of our minds. This seeks to identify itself in relation to everything around us in order to understand by accommodating and assimilating the environment. Without a practiced and strong spiritual sense of self, we can confuse our mind's identification with something external as our own personal identity and sense of value. Finally, there is the communal counterpart, which is our connection and identification with our community or family or nation. (This is an extension of our egoic counterpart which identifies with a group and its narrative.)

Each of these counterparts presents a profound challenge, leading to potential unresolved spiritual stagnation, unnecessary suffering, or even evil. But if we can face our counterparts for what they are, we can integrate them into our approach to learning and transformational spiritual growth.

Coping With Our Counterpart

The first reference in the Torah to something that is "not good" comes after creation is apparently complete, when God notes, "It is not good for man to be alone; I will make a fitting helper for him."[41] On the surface, it is not obvious why being alone is not good for man. We might interpret this to mean it is not good for *anyone* to be alone because we are social animals and need the help of others to simply survive as a species, living safely, hunting, harvesting food, and growing families. On the other hand, we might read this statement to underscore the specificity of gender: that it is not good for *men* to be alone. It may then be a warning, since single men do not tend to fare particularly well in society, as shown by an incarceration rate exponentially higher than that of married men.[42]

At this point, it is important not to ascribe blame for the advance of evil to one gender or the other, which is easy to do since the Torah's language is not gender-neutral. Throughout Jewish history, females have taken the brunt of the blame for evil in the world, partly because the serpent seduced Eve, not Adam, and Eve was the first to take the forbidden fruit. Women have paid over and over for this biased reading by being unjustly equated with evil itself. Unfortunately, there is even a rabbinic opinion that goes so far as to say: "As soon as Eve was created, Satan was created with her."[43] Of course, this sexist interpretation of the Torah is abhorrent to many of us and fundamentally unhelpful to our spiritual growth.

However, the rabbinic tradition most often shared in mystical circles reads gender in this story in a completely novel way. It understands "Adam" not as a singular person but rather as a sort of pair of Siamese twins bound in the flesh. This interpretation is derived from the enigmatic final phrase of the verse about the creation of the first human being: "And God created man in His image, in the image of God He created him; male and female He created them."[44] In other words, the strange additional phrase in the Torah, "male and female He [God] created them," specifically implies that the first human being was both male and female at the same time in the same being.

A similar idea is derived from a verse in Psalms which hints that Adam was created with two faces, one in the front and the other in back, one male and the other female. It says, "You formed [or, hemmed] me behind and forward" (Psalms 139:5). Accordingly, when Eve was created, God did not fashion her out of Adam's rib (*tzela*, in Hebrew) as a mere addendum to creation. Instead, this reading understands *tzela* to mean "side," telling of God's essentially cutting this androgynous creature into two distinct beings.[45]

Therefore, Adam and Eve, as distinct male and female counterparts, were created together as one. As opposed to detracting from a complete creature, the creation of Eve was an act of separation, just as in other acts of creation, such as with the upper waters from the lower water and light from darkness. And it is in the separation of Eve that Adam himself is actually created. Consequently, since the moment of separation—masculine and feminine from each other, one end of the spiritual spectrum from the other—the union of male and female is a reunification and return to an original and complete state of wholeness at the time of creation.

The Torah goes on to say that it is from this moment on after her separation from Adam that Eve becomes his fitting helper, his *ezer k'negdo*.[46] However, the translation "fitting helper" does not entirely capture the nuance and power of the Torah's Hebrew. *Ezer k'negdo* is actually a conjunction comprised of several concepts that English translations struggle to articulate. *Ezer* is a noun meaning "a help." *K'negdo* is a bit trickier. Its central component, *neged*, is a transitive verb meaning to face or oppose. Therefore, when Eve was separated from Adam, she became his "help that opposes or faces him"—she became his "counterpart."

This translation is critically important because it is the best rendering the Torah gives of an individual's complete relationship with her or his counterpart. In this literal reconstruction of the term, we see that Eve is no mere helpmate or "fitting helper"; she is something altogether different. Eve is certainly "a help" to Adam but not in any sense of subservience or compliance. They are equals. Her help is defined by the very fact that she opposes or faces him. In other words, unlike in their original Siamese-like state with faces that did not look directly at each other, here, Adam and Eve face one another. Each reflects back to the other, communicating their individual experiences directly. Thus, the help—and, incidentally, the purpose of each party in a relationship—is the act and experience of facing one another.

Facing another person, however, is very difficult. Looking deeply and patiently in the face of another human being is an incredibly intimate moment. It is vulnerable and can be unbearable for some of us. We, therefore, do not do it too often, and, in fact, we are taught at a young age that it is "impolite to stare." In truth, we love to look and stare, but we are not so comfortable when another does it to us because we feel vulnerable and exposed. When someone stares at us, we are confronted with what it must look like to them. We are, in effect, staring at ourselves through their eyes, and if we are uncomfortable with ourselves—not solely our appearance but also our emotional and spiritual disposition—we find ourselves anxious.

Face to face, *panim el panim*, is indeed understood to be the greatest Jewish expression of spiritual intimacy. We see this both when Jacob encounters his counterpart, leading him to be re-named Israel (Genesis 29-31), and at the final moments of Moses's life (Deuteronomy 34:8-10). This is because in the Jewish tradition, the human face—with its forty-three muscles and seven openings—is the single holiest expression of the Divine in the world. What we read in the human face is inimitable, as one need only observe how an infant will be drawn to a face more than any other object. Indeed, the closest we may come to the Divine is the expression in the human face—since we are each created in the image of the Divine. The seven openings resound symbolically with other numerical expressions of the divine nature, such as the seven days of the moon's cycle ending on Shabbat, the seven colors of the rainbow, and seven great lights in the sky: the sun, the moon, and the five visible planets.

The story of Adam and Eve gives us a glimpse into this phenomenon. When Eve is separated from Adam, both she and he are simultaneously created as distinct beings who see one another in this way. Seeing themselves through the eyes of another for the first time likely causes a sense of anxiety and even shame because they are now no longer one. In facing their counterpart, they must face themselves anew.

We learn two significant spiritual principles from this moment in the Torah. First is that this creation happens through separation, just like the creation of light and dark and of the land and the waters. However, on a deeper level, each of these distinct creations is actually one and the same, for they originate from the same one wholeness. The defining feature of their existence is the existence of the other—light is only light because of the dark, and male is only male because of the female.

Second, we learn that creation through separation and distinction is paradoxical. On one hand, the separation and duality leads to a greater understanding of one's parts. On the other hand, however, the separation into distinct parts drives anxiety because it heightens awareness that the separated entities are still inherently part of the same essential, non-dualistic one. Remaining this way yet appearing as separate, distinct creatures is frightening, and at the least, awkward. Separation here is individuation. This leads to comparison, contrast, and judgment, which lead to competition, shame, fear, and anger. Nevertheless, that individuation is only on the material level; it is illusory on the spiritual level. Spiritually, each part emerges from the same origin, and therefore retains a bond with the other. They are counterparts, each a true *ezer k'negdo,* and can exchange information with and know the other on the most intimate level.

Face to Face With Life

In sum, the facing of Eve to Adam and Adam to Eve reinforces the very simple spiritual message that when we look into the eyes of another, we are ultimately looking into ourselves. When we see another—really see another—we also really see ourselves and what it means to be us, as spiritual beings having this human experience.[47] It means that as well as facing our own creative powers, we must face the essential pains of life: our mortality and our inherent imperfections. When we face another, we face our counterpart, and in doing so, we face ourselves and our purpose, which is to confront our existence, to recognize the good and evil in all that is, and to choose the good.

A wonderful and brief summary of this concept comes from a Jewish spiritual teacher who was asked what the world would be like without the existence of evil. He responded by saying that at the dawn of creation, before the separation of Adam and Eve, there was no distinction between good and evil, no distinctions within us as human beings. With the separation, however, there came evil, but also an opportunity for choosing good and for good's triumph over evil. He teaches:

But if there were no evil, there would be no good, for good is the counterpart of evil. Everlasting delight is no delight. That is how we must interpret what we are taught [by the idea] that the creation of the world took place for the good of its creatures. And that is why it is written, "It is not good for man to be alone"—that is to say, the primal Adam that God created "should be alone," without the counter effect and hindrance of the evil inclination, as was the case before the creation of the world. For there is no good unless its counterpart exists. And further on we read, "I will make a fitting helper for him"—the fact that evil confronts good gives man the possibility of victory: of rejecting evil and choosing good. Only then does the good exist truly and perfectly.[48]

When Adam, the first man, the one who came from the dust of the earth, faced Eve, he faced the essence of life itself. After all, the word Eve in Hebrew is *Chava*, which itself means "life."[49] And when Eve, a being of life and giver of life, faced Adam, she faced the dust and the material transitory nature of life. Our task is to integrate our inner Adam and our inner Eve, to accept the reality of our innate division, both the eternal, life-giving force and the mortal reality of existence on this planet as flawed, animal creatures. Man and woman have and are both, and it is in our equal coexistence, both externally with one another and within ourselves, that we reconcile our existence and find healing.

5
The Struggle:
Living as Israel

It is an empirical fact that holiness elevates man, not by
vouchsafing him harmony and synthesis, balance and
proportionate thinking, but by revealing to him the non-
rationality and insolubility of the riddle of existence.
Holiness is not a paradise, but a paradox.[50]
—Rabbi Joseph B. Soloveitchik

As the Book of Genesis progresses from creation through the beginnings of our ancestors, we find the story of Jacob at its heart. It occupies nearly a dozen of the book's fifty chapters. Jacob's story is particularly important for Jewish spiritual identification because he is the father of the Twelve Tribes, and when his name is changed to Israel, he becomes the namesake of the entire Jewish people—the Children of Israel. Names are very important, of course, because one's name is understood to signify one's nature. The name Israel literally means "one who struggles (or wrestles) with God." Therefore, if we take our name seriously, to identify as a Jew in some way implies that part of one's spiritual identity is to struggle.

Jacob's struggle began at his birth. He was born a twin to his brother, Esau, and they were destined to be progenitors of respective nations and worlds. Their twinhood may hearken back to the idea of the first human being as the twin counterparts of Adam and Eve—a single androgynous pair of Siamese male and female twins. In fact, the Torah tells us that even before they were born, Jacob and his twin brother "struggled in [their mother's] womb."[51] He was so embroiled in his struggle that when he entered the world, Jacob "emerged, holding on to the heel of Esau, and so they named him Jacob"[52]—*Yaakov*, which is derived from the Hebrew root *ekev*, meaning, "heel."

As they grew up, Esau, the slightly older brother, is the favored son of his father. Esau is a hunter and outdoorsman. He is the epitome of masculinity, hunting and providing food, and is the rightful heir of the family. Jacob is the opposite. He is his mother's son. Jacob is an *ish tam*, a simple man or, as the Torah put it, "a mild man who dwelled in the tents."[53] Jacob's adolescence, however, is in many ways defined by his attempts to resemble his brother. He works to provide food like his brother by cooking lentil stew; he puts on the clothes of his brother with skins of hair; and he takes his brother's blessing from his aging, blind father, Isaac. Jacob could not actually be his older brother Esau, the strong and favored one, so he spent his early days trying to be just like him.

After he pretends to be Esau, deceiving his aging father, Isaac, and stealing Esau's rightful blessing, Jacob is forced to flee for fear that Esau will exact revenge. He follows his mother's advice about where to go and finds himself living with his uncle and future father-in-law, Laban. In many ways, the experience with Laban reflects back to Jacob the deceit and manipulation that he himself employed with his father and brother. Laban manages to keep Jacob off-balance. Instead of dwelling in tents as he did earlier, Jacob, now with Laban, dwells mostly in confusion. Laban promises him Rachel, but instead he gets Leah. Laban makes an agreement that Jacob will work for seven years, but he ends up working for fourteen. The world becomes very complicated as Jacob grows into adulthood; perhaps he forgets that he is an *ish tam*, a simple or mild man.

At this point in his story, we can see that Jacob grows into a man in a challenging world, and his identity is primarily defined by what he lacks and by not getting what he wants. He was second born (by only seconds), but that was not enough. He had Leah, but she was not enough because he really wanted Rachel. Living with Laban, growing in prosperity, acquiring more property and women to bear his children was also not enough. At this stage, Jacob seems to lack an authentic sense of his own self. He seems to be chasing the person ahead of him, and, apropos of his name, *Yaakov*, he is always trying to grasp at that person's heel.

Jacob's experience mimics the lives of many contemporary young people as he grows into the world without knowing what he wants. All he knows is that he wants something else—that what he is, and what he has, is not it. His internal life is characterized by ups and downs, like the angels on the ladder in his dream,[54] which marked the start of his journey away from home, into exile.

Crossing the River

Caesar crossed the Rubicon, Washington crossed the Delaware, Moses walked through the Sea of Reeds, and Joshua crossed the Jordan. Abraham is given the designation as the first Hebrew, or *Ivri*, literally meaning "one who crosses over," because he crossed the Euphrates River from his Mesopotamian homeland into the land of Israel. So often in stories, the moment of redemption or resolution happens when crossing a river. Jacob is also tasked with crossing a river in order to return to his native land. Crossing a river in mythology and epic poetry symbolizes passing over a spiritual threshold, from one state of being to another, and it is often challenging and comes with a cost. For Jacob, the river he must cross certainly suggests a personal threshold, as it is practically his own name, *Yavok*—echoing *Yaakov*.

On one side of the river, his home country and his brother, Esau, await him. On the other side is his family and all of the wealth he has acquired. Jacob is frightened of his brother and the potential revenge he might exact because of Jacob's deception so many years ago. He decides to divide his camp to minimize casualties if Esau attacks. He sends Esau gifts to appease him, and prays to God for mercy and deliverance. Then, during what was likely a sleepless night, Jacob awakes and sends his wives, handmaids, and children across the dry river. Then, oddly, Jacob goes back across the river alone, perhaps to retrieve any remaining possessions.[55] Nevertheless, Jacob finds himself all alone … or was he? The Torah mysteriously states: "Jacob was left alone. And a man wrestled with him until the break of dawn."[56]

There, alone in the darkness, Jacob finds himself confronted with a mysterious man. The Jewish tradition tries to comprehend how Jacob could both be alone and yet wrestle someone else. The Torah implies that Jacob believed the mysterious man to be some sort of supernatural, supernal being. After all, Jacob will soon name the place *Peniel*, meaning "The Face of God," proclaiming, "I have seen a divine being face to face, yet my life has been preserved."[57] The rabbinic commentators suggest that this divine being is actually Esau's guardian angel.[58] The rabbis seem to be suggesting that Jacob, in his lifelong struggle with his brother, is not yet ready to face the real Esau in person. First, Jacob must resolve with himself what might be the image of his brother, the image he had always pursued and imitated.

Several modern rabbis and commentators offer a third possibility—that the mysterious "man" with whom he wrestled was none other than Jacob himself. The Hebrew word in the verse, *va-yivater*, translated as "And he was left," in the sense of left alone, is used only one other time in the Torah, when Abraham makes a pact with God through an animal sacrifice, in which he splits the pieces of the animals into parts.[59] It is known as the Covenant of the Pieces, and the word's meaning in that context is "to split." Therefore, applying this alternative rendering to Jacob's story, it is not just that he was left alone but also that he was split off in some way, or, more specifically, experienced himself as split. That is to say, at the moment of his return home and reckoning with his brother, Jacob, the twin who split from his brother, is now internally split, with the opposing sides of himself wrestling one another.

Internal Splits

Many of us may relate to feeling split. We feel divided over what life presents us with, and, like Jacob, we can feel caught alone, wondering how to navigate the rapids of life's winding river. Primarily, we are pulled in two directions: toward what is good and toward what is bad. These poles become complicated, however, because the difference between them is often hard to see. What looks or feels good may not actually be good, and what looks bad may not actually be bad. Sometimes what we want for ourselves is actually bad for us. We want to relax, but we need to work. We want pleasure, but the pleasure we seek may be unhealthy or dangerous. We want to feel free to do what we want, but there are rules to follow. We want to feel strong and healthy, but we get sick and feel weak. We want to feel confident and fearless, but we get scared. We want fairness and justice, but life is often unfair and unjust.

Thus, we are caught on a narrow bridge between two opposing poles. Judaism teaches that each of us contains these poles within our own psyches as impulses or urges. We have the inclination and capacity for both good— *yetzer ha-tov*—and bad—*yetzer ha-ra*. It may be easiest to define these by drawing from the great psychoanalyst Erich Fromm:

> Good . . . is the affirmation of life, the unfolding of man's powers. Virtue is responsibility toward his own existence. Evil constitutes the crippling of man's powers; vice is irresponsibility toward himself.[60]

The *yetzer ha-tov* inclines us to affirm our own existence in this place, time, and body through living to our greatest potential. Acting in life-affirming ways or performing "esteemable acts" is an expression of our virtue.[61] On the other hand, the *yetzer ha-*

ra inclines us toward denying our existence in this place, time, and body through living to our lowest potential. Life-denying acts and self-destructive behavior are our vices.

Living with both of these inclinations and knowing we have them within us is a cause of great angst. In fact, one might say that as beings who have "eaten" from the Tree of the Knowledge of Good and Bad, we realize that we are capable of doing bad as well as good. The angst, struggle, and internal suffering we experience is often a result of knowing we are inclined to both good and bad, and that we must watch ourselves fail, succeed, and even consciously choose the bad.

The story of Jacob and Esau is a classic drama of twins, or counterparts, or opposing faces which we see in spiritual accounts over and over. They represent the opposing dualities experienced in life between ourselves and others, but even more so, ultimately, within ourselves. Rabbinic commentaries on Jacob's great and mysterious wrestling match are replete with interpretations of such dualities.

They see Jacob and Esau as metaphors, ranging from the great historical oppositions between the Jewish people and other nations to the opposing forces of human nature, such as between material, bodily desire and spirituality, between the masculine and the feminine, between childhood and adulthood, and, generally speaking, between the *yetzer ha-ra* and the *yetzer ha-tov*. The Talmud famously claims that each person is equivalent to a world unto himself or herself,[62] and, we might even say, worlds upon worlds. We each have all these swirling splits, dualities, and conflicting energies within, and yet we each are also a single, whole being. The reconciliation between these forces is the struggle and defines the spiritual journey of living as *Israel*.

Choosing Good Over Evil

The concept of opposing sides within each individual is found in many spiritual traditions. It speaks to an enduring human challenge. The story of the twins Jacob and Esau who struggle even within their mother's womb is interpreted by some as a metaphor for this inner battle, as Jacob's wrestling with a mysterious, divine being certainly is also. But of the many questions that emerge about the struggle between our opposing forces within, the most important is how one wins such a battle.

A well-known Cherokee legend that resonates with this question tells of an elder speaking to his grandson about the battle that goes on in every person.

> He said, "My son, the battle is between two 'wolves' inside us all. One is evil. It is anger, envy, jealousy, sorrow, regret, greed, arrogance, self-pity, guilt, resentment, inferiority, lies, false pride, superiority, and ego.
> "The other is good. It is joy, peace, love, hope, serenity, humility, kindness, benevolence, empathy, generosity, truth, compassion, and faith."
> The grandson thought about this for a minute and then asked his grandfather, "Which wolf wins?"
> The old Cherokee simply replied, "The one that you feed."

It is an intriguing story. It rings of Abraham Lincoln's first inaugural address in 1861 when he spoke of "the mystic chords of memory . . . when again touched, as surely they will be, by the *better angels of our nature*." Of course, if there indeed are "better angels" existing in our nature, there must also be worse ones, or demons, just like the opposing wolves within. A possible Jewish equivalent is found in the thoughts we quoted earlier from the *Sefer Mitzvot Ha-Gadol* of thirteenth-century scholar Moses of Coucy, who told of the "bitter war" between the half-angel and the half-brute inside us. "Not until the very hour of death," he wrote, "can it be certain or known to what measure the victory has been won.[63]

For both the Cherokee legend and the Jewish medieval teaching, the battle's winner is determined by the attention a person gives to one side or the other. In the Jewish teaching, the angel resists the brute, striving to train the individual toward healthy practices of study and doing the will of God. In the Cherokee tale, one chooses which "wolf to feed," and whichever side is given more attention prevails. The implication of all this is clear: that living good or bad, in darkness or in light, is a choice we make, and it is certainly a spiritual tenet that resonates. It both offers a common rationale for spiritual practice and observance, and lies at the heart of the psychology of habits.

Viewed more closely, however, one may question whether this approach to choosing good over evil is actually how life works. It would be easy, after all, if adhering to the angel or feeding the good wolf were simply a matter of conscious choice. That would explain why people do evil and destructive things—they simply choose them—and would confirm as absolutes our labels of good and evil, light and dark, angels and demons, thus saving us from the ambiguities, shadows, and grays of life.

But that is not how we all actually experience life. Not everyone who commits a crime, becomes addicted, or harms others experiences these things as choices between absolutes. Most of us want to choose goodness, light, and blessing, but which path is good and which is evil is not always clear in the moment. In reality, we are always living in the shadows.

In rethinking this, it may be better to remove the labels of good and evil altogether, as well as the notion of choosing. In some way, such labels only elevate the struggle, lending it too much power. Although it is true that the presence of evil gives us the opportunity to choose and affirm the good, perhaps there is a good aspect to evil. Perhaps the presence of evil is not so altogether evil. As one Hasidic teaching goes:

> The Divine Presence comprises all worlds, all
> creatures, good and evil. It is true unity. How then
> can it contain good and evil, which are self-
> contradictory? But actually there is no contradiction,
> for evil is the throne of good.

This teaching fundamentally states that evil is not the absence of God or good but rather is a part of God. Therefore, to choose only good is to deny an aspect of God's unity. What we truly seek is wholeness and integration, rather than merely choosing good over evil or light over dark. This wholeness is not perfection in the sense of a pristine or pure light but instead is a merging of light and dark. Wholeness in this vein is about embracing all of what we are and acknowledging that our darkness is as important as our light.

Turning back again to Erich Fromm's definition of good and evil, we see that these are not labels of judgment or value but are either "life-affirming" or "life-crippling." The point is that as opposed to choosing good or bad, seeking wholeness means acknowledging that we have everything we need within us, moving constantly between life-affirming and life-crippling energies. Life-crippling activities are those that compel us to merely look for things we already know, which will only give us the illusion that we are in control of the world, and will feed fear, violence, hate, and sameness. When we pursue life-affirming activities, which is what is natural to the spirit—and is something that changes for every individual all through our lives—we come alive and inhabit our unique gifts. Pursuing life-affirming activities is yet another way to speak of, and perhaps even measure, spiritual growth.

Owning Our Inner Demons

Jacob's internal wrestling match represents one of life's monumental journeys toward spiritual growth. It would be easy to choose a winner and a loser, but in this case, as it is with all of us, the winner and the loser is the same individual. When we win, we also lose, and when we lose, we also win. To grow, we must transcend the categories of winning and losing, and instead accept both sides as part of the single whole. The rabbinic sages certainly say: "Who is strong? One who masters his *yetzer ha-ra*."[64] Yet they do not speak of eliminating or nullifying the *yetzer ha-ra*. That is impossible, for it is a part of us. The only way to master or subdue the *yetzer ha-ra* is to own it, become one with it, and come to know it as any other part of the self.

For Jacob to master his opposing sides, he must become all of who he is, both the good and the bad, for nothing truly can change until it becomes what it is. Not until Jacob is completely Jacob can he then transform and become Israel. Not until he becomes fully Jacob can he truly see Esau as Esau. Until then, Esau will just remain the projection of what Jacob wants to see him be.

As we grow spiritually, or as we become and embody Israel, we will struggle with the dark to find the light. And in learning to own that struggle—the struggle marked with pain and shame—we will watch ourselves still choose good. This is the way in which we plant the seeds of resilience. That is to say, though we continue to move through cycles of despair, goodness yet continues to be seen in every dark alley and amid every rocky rapid. Like Jacob in the Torah, we will continue for the rest of our lives struggling, evolving, and further embodying his namesake, Israel, declaring *Hineini*: Here I am, all of me.[65]

6
The Way of
Balance

This is an example of a truthful person as defined by the Talmud: "What is outside is what is inside." A person can be true if he is balanced. If he totally gives or totally restrains himself, he cannot be true. If he is well balanced within himself, however, he can have a balanced relationship with other people.[66]

—Rabbi Aryeh Kaplan

In the nineteenth century in Lithuania, Rabbi Israel Salanter was witnessing a Jewish world taken over by the principles of the Enlightenment. Indeed, with newly found freedoms for Jews and the spread of the universalistic values of the Enlightenment, many Jews left their faith to become assimilated into the general population or even convert to Christianity. Salanter was essentially captured by one question: Why is it so hard to adhere to the principles of the Torah? That is, why is it difficult to remain faithful to Jewish traditions and to do what is good, reinforcing the wisdom of Jewish spirituality and practice in one's life? These are, of course, perennial questions which rabbis and other Jewish thinkers have been constantly asking.

Salanter's question, however, did not lead to a sociological or philosophical answer about his contemporary world but rather to a psychological insight—before Freud's theory of the unconscious and even before there was something called psychology. Although he did not label them the conscious or the subconscious, Salanter understood that there are both "outer" and "inner" processes of thought and emotion. Often, he taught, we are unaware of the inner motivations, desires, and drives that cause us to react or make impulsive decisions. This insight, though it may not entirely explain the historical and religious challenges Eastern European Jews faced in the nineteenth century, paved the way for a new spiritual movement within Judaism, known as *Mussar*.

Mussar, a term drawn from the Book of Proverbs (1:2), refers to a spiritual instruction in moral conduct through which one works to better identify, learn from, and temper those inner motivations and desires. In other words, it teaches, if we can raise our subconscious motivations to the level of our "outer" conscious awareness, we can become able to act with genuine integrity and wholeheartedness. Naturally, this is not simple, leading to systems of study, meditation, and spiritual practice developed to foster such growth.

Alan Morinis of the Mussar Institute explains that the core affirmation of Mussar is that each of us is a holy and pure soul. The problem is that the reality of life's ups and downs can hide the brilliance of our souls so that they lose their true radiance. Mussar, therefore, teaches that through practices such as study, reflection, spiritual accounting, and deeds of lovingkindness, one can elevate the soul to greater consciousness. Ultimately, such uplift results from balancing one's spiritual traits. As Morinis writes:

> The unbalanced soul-traits act as "veils" that block the inner light. The issue is never the inner qualities themselves—Mussar tells us that all human qualities, even anger, jealousy, and desire, are not intrinsically "bad." These traits that we might call vices have their positive role to play in our lives, in the way that anger is an important signal to action in the face of

injustice, or jealousy can be a very motivating inner
force to do good. But when a soul-trait persists
within us in an extreme of either excess or deficiency,
then our innate holiness will be obscured. A trait
that tends toward the extreme at either end of the
spectrum drops down a veil that blocks the inner
light of the *neshama* [soul].[67]

Mussar, accordingly, presents us with what Morinis calls a
"map of inner life" that points to the places in our spiritual disposition that require attention, more equilibrium and balance.
The practice of Mussar offers a curriculum of sorts to identify
the spiritual traits we have that are out of balance and the steps
that will raise our consciousness to correct them and improve.

It is worth noting that this idea of balancing spiritual attributes
is found throughout Jewish literature. Salanter knew he was not
making up the idea, as he clearly drew upon previous material,
including *Mesillat Yesharim* by Moshe Chaim Luzzatto (1707-
1746) and the largest influence on Salanter's ideas, *Cheshbon Ha-
Nefesh* by Menachem Mendel Lefin (1749-1826).[68] Even those
great works, however, are predated by Maimonides (1135-1204),
who taught a similar philosophy of balancing spiritual traits in
his masterful address on ethics known as *Shemoneh Perakim*, or
The Eight Chapters. He writes in Chapter 4:

Good conduct is conduct that is balanced
between two extremes, each of which is unfavorable:
one is excess and the other is restriction. Personal
virtue refers to tendencies and habits that equally
balance between the bad tendencies of excess and
restriction. For one's character traits come from one's
conduct. For example, restraint is the intermediate
quality between indulgence and the lack of any
feelings of desire. Thus, restraint is a positive activity

> . . . . The intermediate path is what is praiseworthy;
> it should be the path to which a person should aspire
> according to which he should direct his conduct.[69]

Although Maimonides does not refer here to the psychological dimension and inner desires that Salanter and Mussar emphasize, he addresses the same spiritual process of identifying those of our personal characteristics that are out of balance. Maimonides suggests that too much or too little of any trait or tendency is spiritually unhealthy, and that therefore we should practice, through our conduct and behavior, to counterbalance that trait until equilibrium is found and virtue emerges. Maimonides calls this the "intermediate path." Furthermore, similar to Mussar, no single personal trait or tendency is necessarily "bad." Rather, negative conduct and poor choices are more likely to occur when these are out of balance.

The concept of balancing our spiritual traits is also not only a Jewish idea. Although there are significant differences between Maimonides and Aristotle, for example, Maimonides' ethic of virtues is very Aristotelian in the sense that it is about following the mean of the virtue itself, which was a central concept of Aristotelian ethics.[70] Lefin's *Cheshbon Ha-Nefesh*, which was so influential at the dawn of the Mussar movement, is based on the personal system of virtuous practice described by Benjamin Franklin in his autobiography.[71]

In the twentieth century, a new spiritual movement known as Alcoholics Anonymous arose which uses an approach to character improvement similar to that of Franklin and Mussar. The Fourth Step of the program's characteristic 12 Steps suggests that participants "made a searching and fearless moral inventory of ourselves." This step asks individuals to take a thorough accounting of their fears and resentments toward institutions and other people. It helps them recognize their own role in their negative or harmful behavior, and where they may have expressed unsavory behavior such as dishonesty, laziness, and false pride. Then, guided by a mentoring sponsor, a person is ideally introduced to his or her spiritual curriculum, noting where the individual may need to work on moral matters such as greater honesty, taking more initiative, or assuming more humility. Here too we see a spiritual approach of identifying and balancing virtues. In 12-Step language, this is referred to as a balance of one's character defects and character assets.

The Spiritual DNA of Balance

Kabbalah, or Jewish mysticism, also presents a system of spiritual balance of character attributes. This is best portrayed in what is known as the *Sefirot*. The *Sefirot*, plural of *sefirah* (literally, "portion"), refer to ten emanations, or aspects of God in the universe. The *Sefirot* play a central role throughout kabbalistic doctrine and teachings, with each *sefirah* embodying a divine quality or virtue. According to Kabbalah, the *Sefirot* are the underlying forces in the world and in the Torah. In this vein, they represent a sort of "spiritual DNA" of the universe, God, and the human spirit.

At the head of the *Sefirot* are three incomprehensible dimensions of God, as well as soul. These are called *Keter*/Crown, *Chochmah*/Wisdom, and *Binah*/Understanding. Below them are seven "lower" or "emotional" dimensions, usually depicted as a vertical chart showing two of the *sefirot* on each side and three streaming down the center.

All are clearly interconnected, and there is an unmistakable balance among the attributes. This balancing of the opposing qualities is the key to understanding how the *Sefirot*, our spiritual DNA, work in our lives.

At the heart of the diagram, often referred to as "The Tree of Life," lies the *sefirah* or attribute of *Tiferet*, which is translated as harmony or beauty, and commonly interpreted as balance. Sitting in the center of the chart, *Tiferet* represents the primary channel through which the flow of God's energy moves from top to bottom and side to side. Indeed, accordingly to Kabbalah, *Tiferet* is the central and most humanly intelligible experience of the divine in this world. *Tiferet*, the attribute of harmony and balance, is the pivot on which our spiritual experience and growth depends.

The way into *Tiferet* is through the two primary *sefirot* feeding it from each side: *Chesed*/Love, and *Din*/Judgment. In other words, we need to integrate love and judgment to achieve harmony and balance; we need both. Love, in and of itself, is certainly wonderful and beautiful. It is what expresses our unbounded interconnectedness. Love is the energy of togetherness, compassion, mercy, kindness, and sharing. It may be what is most worth living for, worth dying for, and, according to many poets, the substantive nature of the human soul. Some even say that God is love.

Despite all of the wonderful things we can say about love, in our "real" world, love without bounds can also be detrimental. Boundless love can lead to stagnation, procrastination, and lack of creativity and ambition. If unbounded love was the only experience we had, we might feel as if we had all we needed, and nothing more would motivate us to go beyond where we are now. We might not be motivated to learn more, experiment, fix, heal, take adventures, and create.

Judgment, or *Din*, is opposite from love on the *Sefirot* chart. It is the attribute of discernment, creating boundaries, and distinguishing differences. Judgment helps us to be critical and to notice where injustices cause harm, where work needs to be done, and where healing and help are demanded. It motivates us out of complacency. Moreover, judgment is how we recognize our own individual differences; it is how we know our gifts and strengths so we can apply them where they are needed most. Judgment also shows us our limitations, expressing itself to us in fear just as much as it does in strength.

Fear, however, is not necessarily a bad thing. After all, it has likely saved many of our lives at one point or another. Fear is a form of judgment and discernment that tells us not to go too far out in the ocean, or not to get into the car with that stranger, or to slow down when we are driving too fast.

Judgment alone, however, can be detrimental. Living life by seeing only differences and being critical is alienating. When we are too judgmental, many of us can feel how it leads to anger, jealousy, self-pity, and general negativity. With too much judgment, we end up all alone, for there is nothing to satisfy us. There is no forgiveness in judgment alone, and it can therefore become a weapon of disparagement.

Interestingly, according to the *Sefirot*, no qualities are designated as bad or evil. Evil is not something that is innate or necessary to the spiritual system. Evil and the *yetzer ha-ra* ("the evil inclination") is actually a byproduct that occurs when the universe or an individual is out of balance. Primarily, it results from too much Judgment or *Din*, and too little Love or *Chesed*. Being too judgmental increases our inclination to be fearful and resentful, which leads to isolating ourselves from the rest of the world, or even sometimes violently lashing out at it because we cannot recognize the love and hope that is also present.

Tiferet is harmonious balance, representing the proper measure of both *Chesed* and *Din*. It is genuine connection and deep care for others, the world, God, and ourselves, while remaining thoughtfully aware of the reality of life with both its pain and its joy. *Tiferet* is expressed by leaning into another or the world with trusting love, while simultaneously maintaining one's own individuality and dignity. Artist and poet Judy Chicago captured this idea of a lived *Tiferet* in her poem "Merger," when she wrote:

> *And then all that has divided us will merge*
> *And then compassion will be wedded to power*
> *And then softness will come to a world that is harsh*
> *and unkind*

And then both men and women will be gentle
And then both women and men will be strong
And then no person will be subject to another's will
   And then all will be rich and free and varied
And then the greed of some will give way to the needs of
many
   And then all will share equally in the Earth's
abundance
   And then all will care for the sick and the weak and
the old
   And then all will nourish the young
And then all will cherish life's creatures
   And then everywhere will be called Eden once
again.[72]

Acceptance Leads to Balance

In his book *Jewish Meditation*, Aryeh Kaplan begins by challenging the reader to simply stop thinking.[73] But is this even possible? In our cerebral, stimulated world of judging and activation, what happens when we try to stop thinking? For most people who try this for the first time, it is incredibly difficult. The mind has its own reverie; it tells stories, repeats thoughts and experiences, rehearses for the future. If we discipline ourselves to stop doing this, we find that we are thinking about stopping thinking, which is not actually stopping. In this world, where so much is out of our control and so much of life is simply given to us, it is interesting that we struggle to control that which is most intimate and personal—our own minds.

Meditation, which has grown in popularity over the past several decades, has long been a Jewish practice. There are Jewish traditions of meditation, generally referred to as *hitbodedut* (literally, "aloneness" or "individual contemplation"), that go all the way back to the time of the Bible. The renaissance of Jewish mysticism in the thirteenth and fourteenth centuries brought on new meditative forms and techniques, which have continued to evolve into the practices of Hasidism today.

One of the simplest meditation techniques is to try to hold the image of a letter, such as "A," in one's mind as long as possible. This is hard to do because other thoughts, impulses, and feelings arise, causing us to "drop" the letter. What we experience instead can be anxiety, concerns about one's schedule, or a nagging, unresolved problem. We may realize that we are worried about finances or a relationship, we may be upset about something someone did or said to us, or we may feel guilty about something we ourselves did or said.

When meditating, we often feel more deeply into our bodies than usual. Forcing ourselves to be still, we may pay more attention to our sore back or stomachache, feelings we would normally ignore to get through the day. We can also recognize the strength and vitality of our bodies. In just a few minutes of meditation, we can experience an integration of our thoughts, feelings, and body. There is much to learn from that which is already within us.

The main purpose of Jewish meditation is transition from what the mystics call "the mentality of childhood" (*mochin de'katnut*) to the "mentality of adulthood" (*mochin de'gadlut*), or from "small mind" to "expanded mind." Many adults go through the day remaining in the "mentality of childhood," and we all do this to a certain degree by being so consumed with our schedules, problems, and appetites that we are unaware of the bigger reality that is right before us. Do we stop to "smell the flowers," so to speak? Do we stay angry or resentful about problems over which we have no control? Do we fantasize in unhealthy ways that contribute to distraction and procrastination? Are we merely reacting impulsively to what is going on or are we truly weighing our choices and responding thoughtfully? Are we seeing the positive in people as much as we are judging them critically?

Meditation and observing our minds helps us to essentially answer the question: Are we accepting life on life's terms? This may be the primary goal of all spiritual practice. But acceptance does not mean resignation or acquiescing, as many people interpret it; in reality, it is the recognition and understanding that most of life is not ours to control. It is seeing reality for what it is rather than denying and fighting it. In fact, denying and fighting with reality may be the definition of insanity, and living in acceptance the quintessential definition of living sanely. Acceptance is truly synonymous with the Jewish notion of *mochin de'-gadlut* or "expanded mind."

One of the best illustrations of the power and importance of acceptance comes from a personal account in the book *Alcoholics Anonymous* (a.k.a., "The Big Book").

> Acceptance is the answer to *all* my problems today. When I am disturbed, it is because I find some person, place, thing, or situation—some fact of my life—unacceptable to me, and I can find no serenity until I accept that person, place, thing, or situation as being exactly the way it is supposed to be at this moment. Nothing, absolutely nothing, happens in God's world by mistake. Until I could accept my alcoholism, I could not stay sober; unless I accept life completely on life's terms, I cannot be happy. I need to concentrate not so much on what needs to be changed in the world as on what needs to be changed in me and in my attitudes . . . .
>
> Perhaps the best thing of all for me is to remember that my serenity is inversely proportional to my expectations. The higher my expectations of people are, the lower is my serenity. I can watch my serenity level rise when I discard my expectations. But then my "rights" try to move in, and they too can force my serenity level down. I have to discard my "rights," as well as my expectations, by asking

myself, How important is it, really? How important
is it compared to my serenity, my emotional
sobriety? . . . .

I must keep my magic magnifying mind *on* my
acceptance and *off* my expectations, for my serenity
is directly proportional to my level of acceptance.[74]

We see here that when we focus on how we want something
to be, we are fighting against the stream of life. As has been said,
"Expectations are resentments waiting to happen," and resentments are poisonous. Instead, we must recognize that our personal expectations and desires are not always in agreement with
God's will or the universe's will. Therefore, rather than trying to
force our will on something immovable and greater than our own
comprehension and power, spiritual growth calls for acceptance.

The flip side of acceptance, however, is recognizing when we
are called to act and take responsibility. Acceptance makes right
action possible because it includes accepting our own strengths
and what we can contribute. Judaism teaches that the world is
not perfect, and there are problems. We are not intended to
stand idly by in response to them, such as when injustice occurs.
We are obligated to pursue justice, rebuking the guilty and helping to the vulnerable. Abraham Joshua Heschel famously ham-
mered home the point that not only do we need God but also
that God needs *us* for these very purposes.[75] As the famous spiritual story goes:

A religious man saw a crippled beggar who had
been horribly beaten. The holy, religious man went
into deep prayer and cried out, "O God, how is it
that a loving creator such as Yourself can bear witness
to such things and yet do nothing about them?"
After a long silence, God replied, "I did do
something about them. I made you."

Straddling the two poles of acceptance—over the things that are out of our control and those that call on us to act and take responsibility—is a lifelong challenge. It is not always easy to know which is which in our day-to-day life. "The wisdom to know the difference," as the well-known Serenity Prayer states, emerges from meditation, reflection, study, and often help from others. Our goal is to be effective when we act and to ensure that we are not simply deceiving ourselves with ulterior and self-centered motives. Maintaining our awareness of these two sides of the question of acceptance is an expression of balance and harmony. Inaction sometimes uses as much energy and strength as acting does. When we are in true acceptance, we can see it in our lives and experience as though we are swimming with the current of life rather than against it—experiencing the integrity of balance within ourselves and in relationship to the rest of the world. We are living with our "inside" in harmony with our "outside."

7
Welcoming in Joy

God is not only the creator of earth and heaven. He is also the One "who created delight and joy."[76]

—Abraham Joshua Heschel

When we think about the Jewish people and Jewish history, we do not tend to think of happiness and joy. Rarely do depictions of the Jewish people that we read describe them as joyful—as opposed, for instance, to "they are small people," "a beleaguered people," or "a hated people." Sure, positive descriptions sometimes characterize them as "a smart people," "an accomplished people," or "a resilient people," but there isn't much about joy. It is as if simply being a part of the Jewish people grants us Ph.D.s in misery and grief.

Even the Torah—the core and centralizing text of the Jewish people—is not a happy and joyful read. All one has to do is start reading the opening stories to get a taste of what kind of book it is. The first two characters, Adam and Eve, are kicked out of Eden and cursed. The first child, Cain, murders his brother. More and more people inhabit the earth only to be filled with corruption and violence, so that God sends a terrible flood destroying everyone and everything, except for one family. This is the start of Judaism's most central and hallowed text. Joy does not leap from the pages.

At certain seasons, though, we are encouraged to increase our joy. On the festival of Sukkot, we sing the Torah's declaration,

V'samachta be-chagekha . . . v'hayita akh same'ach, "You shall re-joice in your festival . . . and you shall have nothing but joy" As on Passover in the spring, during Sukkot in the fall, we remember the Exodus from Egypt and how we narrowly escaped Pharaoh's clutches.

Here again, we see the oddity of Jewish expressions of joy. For holidays that remember the escape from Egypt, the primary rationale for celebration is this: They tried to enslave and kill us; they failed; and so we celebrate! The motif is especially clear for the holiday of Purim, when Jews are instructed to increase their joy.[77] Haman, the bad guy, plotted against us, but Mordecai and Esther upended his evil designs. As the classic joke suggests, all of Jewish history and every Jewish celebration seems to share the same theme: "They tried to kill us, we survived, let's eat." Again, not so joyful.

With all the tragedy that has befallen the Jewish people over the millennia, there seems to be a part of the Jewish psyche—or at least the Jewish identity—that doubts the possibility of happiness and joy. Modern Jewish comedians have captured this perhaps better than anyone else. Actors and writers such as Woody Allen and Larry David embody the stereotypical skeptical, self-deprecating, obsessive-compulsive Jew who is a victim of his own making. The characters they portray do not seem to allow themselves to be happy and joyful. They are always driving themselves crazy, never seeming able to achieve any peace of mind. Furthermore, they are skeptical of other people who are happy, joyful, or content, as if anyone who is happy must simply be naive or ignorant about all the obvious problems in life.

Yet despite this, there is still a deep undercurrent of joy that energizes the foundation of Jewish spirituality. It is layered in a somewhat-paradoxical truth. On one hand, yes, the world is full of problems; it can be dark, painful, bitter, and unfair. Yet on the other hand, none of that darkness actually diminishes the joy in the world. In fact, in some way, the pains of life may actually even give birth to the joy.

The Jewish spirit of joy in this regard is very honest. Judaism does not promise that everything will be fine—everything certainly will not always be fine. However, if we have a level of faith and trust, if we have practiced acceptance and balance, and if we have acknowledged the truth of our own stories, we will recognize that God and the universe has given us the resources and depth of soul to able to go through difficult times and still experience joy. Ultimately, this is a hopeful outlook; it is a grounded, realistic optimism that denies neither pain nor joy and beauty.

This experience of the reality of life and joy is found in the traditional Jewish daily morning meditation from the Book of Psalms:

> O Lord, my God, I cried out to You, and You healed me.
> O Lord, You saved me from the pit of death . . . .
> For God is angry but a moment,
> Divine love is lifelong.
> We may lie down at night with tears,
> But in the morning we sing with joy.[78]

Born of Gratitude

The Jewish tradition asserts that the best way to experience joy is simply to realize the blessings we have been given and to understand that we are overflowing with reasons to be grateful. Consequently, Jewish spiritual practice includes blessings of gratitude at every turn of the day. The first words we are to speak each day are "Thank you." We continue with affirmations and thanksgiving for the body, the soul, the ability to stand and see and think, the opportunity to learn and study, the blessings of community, and so on and so forth until a minimum of a hundred blessings are acknowledged by each person every day. Consider for a moment the world we would have if everyone took it as a serious idea—that we have at least a hundred blessings to be grateful for every single day. Undoubtedly, the result would be a different world. It would be a world guided by gratitude; it would be a world of joy.

The movement from gratitude to joy, however, is not static. There is a flow to it that continuously washes in and recedes. David Steindl-Rast, a Benedictine monk who grew up in Vienna during the Holocaust and has championed interfaith dialogue, presents one of the most luminous descriptions of this process in describing how gratitude and joy are spiritually interconnected:

> The reason why I use the words "gratitude" and "gratefulness" and "thanksgiving" in the way in which I use them is that we really need different terms for our experience. And we all know from experience that moments in which this gratitude wells up in our hearts are experienced first as if something were filling up within us, filling with joy really, but not yet articulate. And then it comes to a point where the heart overflows, and we sing, and we thank somebody; and for that, I like a different term, and then I call that "thanksgiving." And the two of them are two aspects, or two phases actually, of the process that is gratitude . . . .
>
> And this idea of a vessel that is still inarticulate until it overflows, that is also very helpful in another way. It's like the bowl of a fountain when it fills up, and it's very quiet and still. And then when it overflows, it starts to make noise, and it sparkles, and it ripples down. And that is really when the joy comes to itself, so to say; when it is articulate.[79]

Steindl-Rast explains here that our experience of gratitude is one that comes in an inexplicable form of embodied appreciation. That is what he calls "gratitude." The second aspect he describes is our attention to that moment of gratitude, when we actually take notice and realize we are grateful. In that moment, we awaken to beauty, wonder, and goodness that may be present, and we are simply thankful to be alive. That, he calls "gratefulness." Finally, the synchronous occurrence of experiencing gratitude and our awareness and awakening to it leads to our "hearts overflowing" and our subsequent urge to express thanks. That is what he calls "thanksgiving." Such thanksgiving fills the Jewish prayer book and characterizes the quintessential Jewish expression of joyful celebration during lifecycle moments (e.g., births and weddings), the festivals of the year, and each weekly Sabbath.

What is it, however, that elicits that first ineffable moment of gratitude which leads to joy? Rabbi Jonathan Sacks says it may emerge from an embrace of life for life's sake, despite our mortality.[80] Joy, he writes, is an expression of gratitude for life in the moment itself. We may be either consciously or unconsciously aware of the fleeting brevity of our lives; we are continuously uncertain as to how long we have in the world, or even whether we will be remembered. But there are moments, whether from appreciating the beauty of nature, a moving piece of music, the feel of the cool breeze on our skin, or the loving smile of our child, that we are attuned with the universe and thankful to be its witness. For Rabbi Sacks, quoting the great existentialist philosopher, Søren Kierkegaard: "It takes moral courage to grieve; it takes religious courage to rejoice." Sacks adds:

> . . . [J]oy lives not in thoughts of tomorrow but in the grateful acceptance and celebration of today. We are here; we are alive; we are among others who share our sense of jubilation. We are living in God's land, enjoying His blessing, eating the produce of His earth, watered by His rain, brought to fruition under His sun, breathing the air He breathed into us, living the life He renews in us each day. And yes, we do not know what tomorrow may bring; and yes, we are

surrounded by enemies; and yes, it was never the safe
or easy option to be a Jew. But when we focus on the
moment, allowing ourselves to dance, sing, and give
thanks, when we do things for their own sake, not
for any other reward, when we let go of our
separateness and become a voice in the holy city's
choir, then there is joy.

Joy Is Not Happiness

Sacks also points to another great spiritual insight, which is
the difference between joy and mere happiness. He cites the Book
of Ecclesiastes, which is read each year during the festival of
Sukkot. Ecclesiastes essentially presents himself as a man in search
of the good life. He pursues all kinds of pleasures and delights,
only to find himself unfulfilled by the temporary happiness he
finds. The book is littered with wise axioms and quotable
proverbs, yet it is fundamentally a meditation of a man searching
for something deep and meaningful. It is from this that Rabbi
Sacks takes his point that joy arises not from fleeting encounters
with pleasure and happiness but rather from an abiding appreciation for all of life.

Renowned psychologist and Holocaust survivor Viktor
Frankl touches on this distinction in his work. Frankl, whose
story and theory is conveyed in his book *Man's Search for Meaning*, was a firsthand witness to the greatest horrors and atrocities
that humans have endured. Yet as he survived this, he saw a difference in how people coped with the situation. Some people
in the concentration camps were absorbed by despair, hopelessness, and suffering, and would even commit suicide rather than
face the terrors of the Nazis (which is tragically understand-
able). Others, Frankl noted, found ways to continue to persist
in what many would describe as Hell on Earth. They even
found room in their experience for humor, celebration, and
artistic expression.

The difference for those who managed to persevere was that they found some sort of meaning greater than themselves in their suffering and life. After surviving the camps himself and being liberated, Frankl went on to dedicate his career to exploring this phenomenon, calling his psychological work Logotherapy, from "logos," which is Greek for "meaning" (i.e., meaning therapy). Although Frankl did not address happiness at any length, he maintained that in the absence of meaning, people tend to fill their lives with hedonistic pleasures, power, materialism, hatred, boredom, or neurotic obsessions and compulsions, which over the long term lead to discontent and the absence of joy.[81]

Many scholars who study the Greek translation of the Bible point to the distinct words for joy and happiness. Accordingly, the Greek word for happiness often used in the Bible is *makarios*, which is associated with luck or fortune. In this light, happiness may be etymologically linked to what happens, happenstance, or haphazard. There is a sense of external conditions as the cause. In contrast, the biblical Greek word for joy is *chairo*. Rather than the external, *chairo* indicates an inner sense of gladness, a culmination of well-being and deep-seated satisfaction. The language suggests that rather than resulting from favorable circumstances, joy is an experience of assurance, confidence, and recognition of the gifts of life. Thus, happiness is driven by what is happening and can clearly leave as quickly as it comes. But joy lives within us, and although it certainly is experienced in varying degrees, it can remain despite external conditions.

Given all this, one may wonder why we confuse happiness and joy, and why we tend toward external forms of happiness rather than working to cultivate the depth of gratitude and joy that is so much more valuable. The reason so many experience so little of the meaning, gratitude, and ultimately joy that is available to us is our fear of being too vulnerable. Rather than welcoming the potential joy into our lives and experience, we treat it as a scarce resource. As researcher and author Brené Brown writes:

Joy and gratitude can be very vulnerable and intense experiences. We are an anxious people, and many of us have very little tolerance for vulnerability. Our anxiety and fear can manifest as scarcity. We think to ourselves:

• *I'm not going to allow myself to feel this joy because I know it won't last.*

• *Acknowledging how grateful I am is an invitation for disaster.*

• *I'd rather not be grateful than wait for the other shoe to drop.*[82]

Given the pains of Jewish history and experience, it may not be surprising if part of our collective identity is to be hesitant about joy, while "waiting for the other shoe to drop."[83] The importance of gratitude as a practice is that if we can habituate ourselves to opening to all the blessings in our lives, allowing our hearts to overflow and sing and praise and laugh, we are more likely to feel comfortable allowing joy into our experience. Practicing gratitude helps us let go of the need for things to be either all bad or perfect, and to instead accept reality as it really is— yes, with the lows but also with the highs. As Marianne Williamson put it: "Joy is what happens to us when we allow ourselves to recognize how good things really are." It just takes a little practice.

The Joy of Serving

The Jewish tradition is replete with stories, laws, and language for doing good deeds in the world. Accompanying the importance of this is the concept of *simchah shel mitzvah*, or "the joy of the good deed." The underlying assumption is that when one does something for another that is good, the person who is doing it feels good and joyful. "The joy of the good deed" suggests that joy itself is not something we can will to happen, or a direct goal we can achieve, but rather is a byproduct or outcome of doing good. This brings to mind the fact that Jews do not wish each other a "happy new year," as people do for the secular new year. Instead, Jews wish each other a "good year," a *shanah tovah*, not a "happy year," as if to indicate that goodness precedes joy and happiness, and if we are good, joy and happiness will follow.

Many of us know from our own experience that joy follows doing good deeds. Helping another helps to ease the sting of our own self-consciousness, problems, and preoccupations by taking the focus off ourselves alone. Doing good lifts our spirits because we watch ourselves rise to our own moral values, and we can take satisfaction from our contribution to improving the world and helping others. It is noteworthy to point out that Holocaust survivors often become leading contributors to charities, a clear indication that part of the healing from one's own sorrow and tragedy can be found in the joyful experience of doing something good for another.[84] Mark Twain may have put it most succinctly when he said: "The best way to cheer yourself up is to cheer up somebody else."

Abraham Joshua Heschel was a champion in expounding on not only the virtue of doing a good deed but also the joy of doing it. He noted that humans can become trapped in their self-centered ego, causing anguish and capriciousness. Doing good deeds, however, gives us spiritual release from the chains of the ego, letting us connect with something greater than ourselves and to spiritually grow. This, for Heschel, is the quintessential experience of joy and what he describes as spiritual ecstasy and redemption. He describes the joy of a *mitzvah*, a good deed (literally, "commandment"), in his unique poetic philosophical style:

> . . . Jewish experience is a testimony of *simchah shel mitzvah*, "to the joy in doing a mitzvah."

Everyone knows that out of suffering is a way to
Him. Judaism is a reminder that joy is a way to
God. The mitzvah and the holy spirit are
incompatible with grief or despair.

The experience of bliss in doing the good is the
greatest moment that mortals know. The discipline,
sacrifice, self-denial, or even suffering which are
often involved in doing the good do not vitiate the
joy; they are its ingredients . . . .

There is joy . . . in being able to taste heaven in a
sacred deed. There is joy in being able to link to
eternity, in being able to do His will. A rabbinic
principle states that "the mitzvot [plural of mitzvah]
were not given for the purpose of affording
pleasure."[85] Yet pleasure is not the same as joy.[86]

Jewish spiritual growth involves a process in which we over-
come traits such as self-indulgence, arrogance, envy, exploitation,
and hatred. Heschel, along with other Jewish sages and teachers,
contends that the best measure of that growth and of fulfilling
our highest potential lies in doing good deeds. Though spiritual
growth may not be accompanied by happiness or pleasure, it *will*
be accompanied by joy.

The Sacred Smile

Jewish spirituality is an active expression, and it can be found
anywhere. No place or condition seems to be off limits for spiritual learning and growth. Talmudic and Hasidic stories abound
with lessons learned from the most unexpected and outrageous
places, including the saloon, the bedroom, and even the outhouse.[87] In such situations, these stories demonstrate the vulnerability of our human condition, which may make us wince but
mostly laugh. Indeed, humor and laughter is a healthy part of
Jewish spirituality and certainly of a joyful life. Joy and laughter

is what spiritual writer and essayist Anne Lamott calls, "carbonated holiness."[88]

There is no better way to measure the light and joy in a person's life than one's facial expression, especially when it is punctuated with a smile. A pleasant facial expression is actually deemed a *mitzvah* or good deed in Jewish law.[89] Jewish sages millennia ago anticipated what modern science has recently corroborated. As psychologists tell us today, smiling improves our health by releasing endorphins and neurotransmitters that lower blood pressure as well as reducing anxiety and depression. Moreover, smiling is contagious, symbiotically causing others to relax and become less anxious. It is no wonder that smiling for a photograph is the recommended way to bring out one's best features.

Humor and laughter have been hallmarks of Jewish identity and culture in the past century. Perhaps this comes out of Jewish resiliency and coping with the pains of Jewish history—the maxim that "laughter is the best medicine"—or perhaps it is because even jokes can contain a bit of "Torah." As Heschel said, "Even lowly merriment originates in holiness."[90] Whatever the reason, part of Jewish spirituality is expressed in our ability to laugh at ourselves and life. Humor is among the pantheon of expressivity that helps us to connect to one another through our humanity. One folk story tells of Dovidl, son of the famous Rabbi Zevi Elimelech of Dinov and himself a Hasidic rabbi with many ardent disciples.

> On every Sabbath and also on Holy Days, Rabbi Dovidl refrained from the time-honored custom of expounding on the Torah as he sat in the midst of his disciples. Instead, he diverted them with merry tales and jokes, and everybody, even the graybeards, would laugh heartily.
>
> Once, Rabbi Yichezkel Halberstam was paying him a visit and was amazed at Rabbi Dovidl's odd

carryings-on. "Whoever heard," he began indignantly, "that a *tzaddik* [a righteous person] should behave in such an outrageous way? A fine thing indeed to celebrate God's Sabbath with nonsense, funny stories, and jests! Really, Rabbi Dovidl, you ought to feel ashamed of yourself! Come now, expound a bit of Torah for us!"

"Torah!" exclaimed Rabbi Dovidl. "And what do you suppose I've been expounding all this time? Believe me, Rabbi, there's God's holy truth in all stories and jests!"[91]

Certainly, context and timing are critical to the appropriateness of a good joke or funny story. The key is that humor and laughter allows us to let down our guard, step outside ourselves, and relax. If we take ourselves or even our tradition too seriously without any levity, we run the risk of forgetting our fundamental humanity. Humor and humanity go hand in hand:

The Goldberg family was having Friday night dinner at the house of their grandmother, Bubbe Adella. Seated at the table, little Moishe Goldberg dug into the food immediately.

"Moishe!" his mother exclaimed. "You have to wait until we make the blessing."

"No, I don't," the boy replied.

"Of course you do," his mother insisted. "We always say a blessing before eating at our house."

"That's at our house," Moishe explained, "but this is Bubbe's house. She knows how to cook."[92]

In a revolutionary vein, Jewish spirituality claims that smiling, joy, and making someone else smile with joy may rank among the holiest of endeavors. This one last Talmudic story is understood to be a particular favorite of the Baal Shem Tov, the founder of Hasidism:

> Rabbi Beroka used to visit the marketplace, where the Prophet Elijah often appeared to him. It was believed that he appeared to some saintly men to offer them spiritual guidance.
>
> Once Beroka asked the Prophet, "Is there anyone here who has a share in the world to come?"
>
> "No . . . ," the Prophet started to reply.
>
> But then, as they were conversing, two men passed by, and Elijah remarked, "These two men have a share in the world to come."
>
> Rabbi Beroka approached the men and asked, "What is your occupation?"
>
> "We are jesters," they replied. "When we see men depressed, we cheer them up."[93]

8
A Suggested Program for Spiritual Growth

We should devote our lives to repentance, self-transformation, and yearning to serve God fully. Just imagine: If a person dies and then looks for a way that his soul might return to this world, even for one day—he would work, devoted to Torah, mitzvot, and good deeds on the one day that was given to him as if it were his whole life.... How precious would this day be, since you will never have it again![94]

—Rabbi Shlomo Rabinowich of Radomsk

One of the challenges in our lives is overcoming the power of labels. Once we apply a label to something, whether it is a thing or an idea or a people, we run the risk of objectifying that which we have just named. The label can diminish, denigrate, and deaden the essence and spirit of that which we are discussing. For many in our contemporary world, "religion" has become a highly triggering label. It signifies many different things to different people, pressing political, social, and personal nerves. For some, religion represents the old and the past, rather than the new and the future. That can be good or bad, or both, depending on one's point of view. Religion can represent institutionalism, symbolized by the church or synagogue and all of their rank and file. Again, one's taste may vary as to whether that is a good or bad thing.

"Spiritual" has also become a label. When we speak of something spiritual, what are we talking about? Most likely, we know people (perhaps even ourselves) who identify as "spiritual but not religious." Some of us may also know people who identify as religious but not so much as spiritual. For some people, spirituality is found in nature or in personal meditation. For others, it is found in charity. Some just view the whole idea of "spiritual" as nonsense.

Judaism is a spiritual path that does not fit tightly into any one label. Viewed in this way, spiritual is simply a reality of our experience and the world. From the Jewish perspective, spirituality may be compared to health—we have it. Like health in the bodily sense, spiritual health is an innate fact of our being. And, like bodily health, our spirituality may be life-sustaining and nourishing or not. Like bodily health, our spirituality is something we need to maintain and care about for it to benefit us. Therefore, from the Jewish perspective, the question is not *whether* something is spiritual but rather *how* it is spiritual.

"Religion" is not an originally Jewish term or idea. In fact, the Hebrew word for "religion" (*dat*) largely came into use only in the early twentieth century, when modern Hebrew began to be spoken in Israel. Until then, Jews predominantly referred to their religious identity as being part of a nation of people who lived by the Torah—in other words, that it was more of a code of living or way of life.

Today, especially in the Western world, religion is often understood as a set of one's personal beliefs in God; it is a synonym for faith. That is not Judaism. Faith and how one expresses her or his faith in God is a part of Judaism but not nearly all of it. When we say Judaism is a religion, we mean something altogether different.

First, Judaism is a religion in the sense that it is based on the claim that life is infinitely meaningful and spiritual. Each of us is made of both stardust and the divine sparks of infinity. Everything we do is meaningful, and we are bound together, all of us, as ripples in the sea of God's infinity of energy and love. This spirituality, though, is not Jewish; God is a not a Jew. I may be a Jew. We may be Jews. Our communities may be Jewish communities, yet everything we do is shaped by and reflects the fact that we are human beings on this planet in relationship with a God that is as vast and infinite as the cosmos. There are many paths to God in our human experience, and all paths are divinely chosen in their own way. Thankfully, Judaism is a deeply wise one.

Another way Judaism can be understood as a religion is in the way that the twelfth-century scholar Maimonides described it. In his *Guide for the Perplexed*,[95] he defines religion when he argues on behalf of two religious endeavors: *tikkun ha-nefesh* and *tikkun ha-guf*—fixing the soul and fixing the body. And by the body, he means fixing the world. In other words, Judaism invites us to inculcate into ourselves and others a deep spiritual and emotional openness, and engage in activities and rituals that foster personal meaning. Jews are also asked, however, to see to it that the realm of the body—the world here and now—is healthy, by ensuring that we feed each other, clothe each other, and take care of each other and the planet. *Tikkun ha-nefesh* seeks to make people better people, and *tikkun ha-guf* seeks to make the world a better world. And if an action is not both healing the self and healing the world, Judaism is simply not interested.

Judaism may, therefore, be understood as a religion in the etymological sense of the word. Religion comes from the root *lig*, meaning to connect. Hasidism advanced this understanding of Judaism when it linked the Aramaic word for "connection"—*tzavta*—with the Hebrew word for performing a Jewish practice, good deed, or ritual—*mitzvah*. The rabbis explained that since the words share nearly the same letters and sound, we learn that performing a religious act is a form of connection. In short, the aim of Jewish spiritual practice and growth is to connect the individual with God, with others, and with herself or himself.

The Value of a Spiritual Program

Many of us find value in what we might refer to as our routine. This can be a healthy endeavor by giving our lives a structure and consistency that both ensure we accomplish what we seek to and provide meaning to our lives. Many studies show that consistent routine and habit also help to maintain proper amounts of sleep, prevent us from indulging in more-destructive behaviors, free up creativity, and bring balance and harmony. Moreover, routine is something with which we can measure our progress and growth.

Routine, however, can also become ordinary and stale. To benefit us most, a routine demands space for improvisation while still adhering to our principles. As Yehudah Aryeh Leib Alter of Ger, known as *Sefat Emet*, writes:

> Habit makes things seem natural and ordinary, and this sense of "nature" hides the inner light [of the act]. This is true even of studying Torah and performing the commandments: When we do them out of habit alone, they become our nature, and we forget their inward meaning. Therefore, we need always seek out some new counsel.[96]

Rather than using the word "routine" for structuring our time and activities, educators, coaches, and even spiritualists often prefer to use the term "program." The important distinction between the two terms is intentionality. Routine can denote a sense of mindlessness, while program seems to emphasize moving toward a goal. Thus, if our intention is spiritual growth, program is more appropriate. (In fact, one could easily argue that the Jewish legal system of *Halakhah*, which is comprised of hundreds of *mitzvot*, is actually a program for spiritual living.) So how then do we define a program?

A program is a set of behaviors and experiences intended to achieve a desired result.

This definition and our aspiration toward spiritual growth mean that we must work backward. In other words, before choosing our set of behaviors and experiences, we must identify the desired result.

As we consider this goal, many varying and perhaps paradoxical ideas may arise. We might consider, for example, serenity, positivity, healthy living, and commitment to Jewish observance—all worthwhile ideas. For the purposes of this book, though, I will suggest another desired result for spiritual growth. It is simple, merely three words: *peace of mind.*[97]

At first glance, this may seem to be more an expression of Eastern religious philosophy than of a Western one. But that hearkens back to the problem of labels. As Judaism has evolved as a spiritual path over the past two millennia, it has traveled through scores of countries and been filtered through an even larger number of languages and cultures. It is difficult to reduce Judaism to a Western or Eastern religious philosophy. Furthermore, our understanding of peace of mind may depend on one's own concept of the self, the mind, and the world. In the context of creating a program of spiritual growth, the elements of the program itself will be the best indicators of what peace of mind really means. Undoubtedly, though, peace of mind is absolutely and unequivocally as Jewish an idea as it is a part of any other culture.

Again, each of us needs to develop our programmatic elements—our set of behaviors and experiences—to meet our own desired results for ourselves, as we each need to see ourselves and our lives connected with care to what we set ourselves out to do. The following is a suggested Seven-Point Program for Spiritual Growth.

First, however, let us digress for a moment to reflect on the number seven, as there is meaning associated with it. In the Jewish tradition, seven is the number symbolically associated with nature and this world. There are the seven days of Creation, seven days of the week, and the shemitah year (the seventh year when agricultural lands are rested). There are also seven "lower" and emotional dimensions to the Kabbalistic Sefirot, seven weeks of Counting the Omer (the days between the festivals of Passover, which celebrates national freedom, and Shavuot, celebrating the giving of the Torah at Sinai), and, as mentioned in an earlier chapter, the seven openings of the human face.

Interestingly, psychology also considers seven to be a "magical" number.[98] Research shows a correlation between seven and short-term memory, in that people can hold seven items in their memory (+/-2) before they begin to lose track. (Perhaps, that is why there are typically seven digits in a phone number, and it is used as a mnemonic for so many things, including the seven seas, seven primary colors, seven wonders of the world, and the seven deadly sins.) For all these reasons and more, seven is an appropriate, meaningful, and memorable value to apply to our suggested program.

Seven Steps to Spiritual Growth

Jewish spiritual growth demands action, as well as personal understanding and intention. As the Israelites declared on receiving the Torah at Mount Sinai, *na'aseh v'nishma*, "we shall act and we shall understand" (Exodus 24:7). A complete program for spiritual growth therefore calls for both structures of behavior and activity, and opportunities for reflection and understanding. Each element of the program will ideally include some sort of *keva*, structure and practice to follow, as well as *kavanah*, intentional direction with which to focus our thoughts. Here are the seven elements I would suggest for a path toward spiritual growth leading to peace of mind.

1. Study—*Talmud Torah*
2. Prayer/Meditation—*Tefilah*
3. Reflective Transformation—*Teshuvah*
4. Service—*Tikkun*
5. Communal Connection—*Kehilah*
6. Exercise and Nutrition—*Shemirat Ha-Guf*
7. Recreation—*Hit'chadshut*

Study—*Talmud Torah*

Of all the Jewish practices, study (or *Talmud Torah*) stands above the rest as the most discussed and revered. As the Talmud famously declares, "The study of Torah is greater than all other *mitzvot* (good deeds) put together."[99]

But no one needs to read the Talmud to understand the significance of Torah study in Judaism. One can simply attend a Saturday morning synagogue service to see the reverence attending the storing, parading, and reading from the Torah.

The Torah is revered in this way because all other Jewish teachings and values are derived from it—the "garden around the Torah." In fact, when we refer to Torah study, we are speaking of not the five books of the Torah alone but also all the connective literature and teachings that the Torah has inspired. "Torah study" is therefore a broad term referring to the Jewish learning that is associated with the Torah and Hebrew Bible itself as well as to the wisdom and practices that descend from it.

Let us look at the question of why Torah study might be a spiritual practice in and of itself. What is it exactly about study that offers us such opportunity for spiritual growth? Learning Torah is not merely recounting names, places, and laws. In the educational world, Torah study can be said to pivot on the highest of objectives—analysis, synthesis, and evaluation—in Benjamin Bloom's famous taxonomy of the six domains of learning. But this does not result from the fact that we are studying, or even what we are studying, but rather from the manner in which we study. *The Jewish approach to how we study is itself the means by which our intellect grows and our spirits are moved.* We can gain access to the spirit by how we use and focus our intellects.

Study is meant to inspire questions. Learning has the power to stir something deep within us that is percolating and waiting to rise. We each have an unquenchable fire inside, and it is from these sparks that questions are born, grow, and then ascend to our consciousness, messengers to the intellect from the soul.

"Coming up" with a good question affirms that fire within, one that burns but does not consume.

When we identify a question that has arisen from within, we are motivated to seek the answer. This is where the terms "*midrash*" and "*derash*" come from (*d.r.sh.*—meaning, "to search"). What are we seeking? Truth. And when we discover even a kernel of truth in our search, even if it's not the complete answer, there is no better affirmation of the spirit. It imbues us with a greater sense of self—more self-esteem and self-knowledge. This is not pride but a sure course of personal healing and growth in self-love, for once this learning process is complete, it gives us a new appreciation for life and all its nuances.

In their immense wisdom, the rabbis realized that study provokes questions which fuel the development and evolution of the spirit. And questions are the most tangible way of evaluating whether we care about something. Not asking questions is a sign that we do not care, and not caring is a sign of the decay of soul.

Of course, the beauty of Torah and rabbinic literature is that they abound in questions. There are so many to be asked about life and the human purpose on Earth that we can generate new ones with each encounter. The possibility of discovery is endless, and, in fact, often requires study of other disciplines, such as history, science, and philosophy, to arrive at the truth. The Torah ("the Tree of Life"), as well as the rabbinic expositions ("the Garden") that surround it, binds the Jewish people together from the ends of the Earth. In our lifelong commitment to study, we unearth our spiritual history while continuing to explore our spiritual destiny. The study of our tradition and all else that feeds the internal fire extends all the way to heaven and to every other Jew who has ever been and ever will be. It is truly the way we continually recongregate at Sinai.

Prayer/Meditation—*Tefilah*

What is it that we fear most? Is it that we are afraid of losing our sense of self? Is it that we are afraid of dying? Our greatest fear is losing our sense of connection. We fear floating aimlessly in the abyss, entirely and utterly alone. In a way, such loneliness and disconnection is a sort of death, since living is essentially connection. As Rabbi Harold Schulweis said, "It is not that I am afraid of dying, it is that I am afraid of never having truly lived."[99] And what does truly living mean if not genuinely engaging one's authentic self with others, with the world, and with God? When we strip down to the core of our being beneath flesh and mind—when we are left with nothing but existence itself and the angst that often accompanies it—we find ourselves alone in prayer. And for Judaism, there is no explicit distinction between prayer and meditation; they are overlapping terms that make one unified process. I will simply refer to them as "prayer."

Real prayer is not language or speech. Real prayer cannot be rote. Prayer is a stretching and reaching out of the spirit to connect in love. Simply put, some experiences are so powerful, so awe-inspiring, that we cannot bear them alone. We feel it in the awesomeness of becoming a parent. There is exhilaration, a deep gratitude, and a humbling fear to the experience. We also feel it when we hit bottom, or experience loss in some other way. There is utter powerlessness, devastating anguish, and a humbling fear. So too in this state of being, from our loneliness, we yearn to reach out and connect. It is a compulsion that is both the need to pray and prayer itself. The act of praying is putting form and expression to the urge that is already inside.

We do not, however, have to experience such earth-shattering highs or lows to have the impulse to connect. We actually experience it all the time because life as a human being is inherently awe-inspiring. But unfortunately, we are all experts at denying it. We are very talented at distracting ourselves with the social drama and politics of the day. And in our technologically oriented world, we are especially adept at distracting ourselves with "stuff"—our cars, computers, smart phones, and televisions. The mind loves to be at work figuring out the puzzles of our contemporary world, and is happy to be given more and more to occupy it. Meanwhile, the soul— denied its need for expression and connection—grows stagnant and begins to decay.

Prayer in this light is a striving for connection. Yet it is also a self-reflective act, and in this way may be what we often call meditation. While we reach out, we look back at ourselves; we seek a witness to affirm our living experience even as we are witnessing it ourselves. Prayer, therefore, is not merely begging and requesting, as the English term implies. In Hebrew, prayer is *tefilah* from the word *lehit'palel*, a reflexive verb literally meaning to judge or act as witness to one's self. As we strive to connect with one another while simultaneously being aware of our own experience, the invisible mental and emotional walls that separate us begin to crumble. We are able to see ourselves alive in our most natural and vulnerable state; we see ourselves through God's eyes.

There are three primary relationships to which we seek to connect in prayer and meditation. First, we strive to gain a better sense of self, the sense of "I" that lets us be whole in the world. As Hillel famously said, "If I am not for myself, who will be?"[100] Traditionally, the first thing Judaism asks us to do in the morning upon waking, the first expression we make at the start of life each day, is to say: "*Modeh Ani* . . . . Thank You, God, for restoring my soul to me with compassion and great trust." In other words, we say, "Thank you for giving me what is uniquely me." We need to say this because each day we have to know that at the very moment of consciousness, we are the most beautiful beings on earth. We are human, children of the Source of All Life, God's greatest accomplishment. Just think of how awesome it is to be a human—all the things we do with our minds and our hands and our hearts. We have infinite value, and we must know it. If we do not affirm our infinite worth and inherent divinity every single day, we are left un-whole.

The great teachers of Jewish mysticism taught that each day when we wake up, we rise again to our own unique *tikkun* (service), our own individual purpose in the world, in partnership with the divine. Each of us has our own unique *tikkun* to fulfill, which we reengage every day. The letters in the word *tikkun* can be rearranged to spell *tinok*, which means child or baby—reminding us that when we wake each day, it is as if we are born again as children to our unique potential and purpose. In other words, the same energy that was in the world when we came into being is there again each day, and we have the innate power to use it to heal ourselves and the world.

Second, we strive to connect with You. That is the You with a capital "Y"—God. Just a sense of "I" is not enough for us to be whole and feel connected. We need a sense of You for the sake of humility in the world. Immediately after Hillel said, "If I am not for myself, who will be," his next sentence was, "But if I am only for myself, what am I?" We need the perspective of God to whom we can defer and whom we can revere and honor. We need God to ask for forgiveness and to confess our sins. We need a You to thank for all we have been given, and to express our requests and needs for ourselves and for others.

Having a sense of You, a sense of God, however, does not mean that we are constrained or pressed beneath God's thumb, so to speak. We can think and believe freely in Judaism and still have behavioral unity. We conform our behavior with standards because there are things that we must do or must not do. That is how we make community and live civilly. We can make community happen, for example, not because we all agree and have the same faith but because we all take the same day off: Shabbat. We have the same holidays, we have the same eating customs, we marry the same way, we bury loved ones and mourn the same way, we all learn the same language (Hebrew), and we are all held to the same moral standards. The idea that we have behavioral unity comes from that sense of You—of Other. It gives us a sense of commandedness and belonging, which humbles us but also empowers us to do the right thing.

And finally, the third point of connection we endeavor to establish is the relationship with community—our place of belonging—a connection of Us. First, we acknowledge the infinite value and beauty of the self. Second, we acknowledge the awe and grandeur of You—a power greater than ourselves. We are grateful for the gift of these perspectives, and with our gifts and human freedoms, we acknowledge that we also must be responsible with such freedoms. And so we turn to community. We ask: What kind of community shall we have? What kind of schools should educate our children? What kind of neighborhoods should we build? What kind of house shall we erect together? Will we be welcoming and respectful? Will we be generous with our time and money? After all, we are inseparable, so what makes us "us"? In this way, prayer reminds us of our own responsibility and role in partnering to improve the world. Heschel points out that beyond the awe of the divine, the purpose of prayer is not to beg God for salvation but to inspire us to look to our communities and to work to make the world a better and more-just place: "Prayer may not save us, but prayer may make us worthy of being saved."[101]

The union of self and God cannot be complete without acknowledging the interconnectedness we have with all others on Earth. We simply cannot be spiritually free ourselves if others are enslaved; we cannot be spiritually sated when we see others go hungry; we cannot be spiritually at home when we see others who have no home; and we cannot be at peace when violence is present. Judaism teaches that we cannot truly rest by standing idly by; to connect we must supply connection.

Prayer therefore consists of gaining a greater sense of *I*, *You*, and *Us*—or really, Self, God, and Community. It is something we need every day because we must remind ourselves every day of the connections that affirm our existence and self-worth. Indeed, this is self-healing.

Reflective Transformation—*Teshuvah*

There are those who believe that nothing ever truly changes, that life is a circle which merely repeats itself in different forms.

These people believe no one actually changes, and that history is doomed to repeat itself. That, however, is not the spiritual approach of Judaism. History is not doomed to repeat itself, neither in our own personal lives nor as a species. Rather than a circle, Judaism believes that life spirals upward ever closer to the divine, ever improving and moving toward more wholeness and goodness. We are not degrading, falling further away from the holiness of the past or from God's revelation at Sinai, but, in fact, we are closer than ever before. Judaism is a spirituality of optimism, and the mechanism on which this spiritual progression advances is *teshuvah*, or repentance.

Teshuvah, from the verb root meaning "to return," is the process by which spiritual change and transformation happens. When this occurs in our characters, we change our behavior and can repair things we have done in the past. That is to say, we cannot change the facts of what was done in the past, but we can change the meaning of the past through what we do in the present. We may have come up short in the past, but if in the end, we come clean and emerge on top of life, the past becomes a stepping-stone to success rather than ending in failure. This is the way it must be, after all, since if we could not change and our character was hopelessly trapped by its early development and past deeds, what point would there be to the future? As the Hasidic master Rabbi Nachman of Bratzlav rhetorically asked: "If we are not better tomorrow than we are today, then why have tomorrow?"

The first thing to know about *teshuvah* is that it is an action, not a thought or feeling. Sure, we could be sorry for past deeds and think we would like to change, but until we do something about it, we have not actually done *teshuvah*. Thinking we are sorry and doing something about feeling sorry have inherently different spiritual values. It is in the act itself of making amends or doing something differently that others and we ourselves see the change of mind manifest in the world, which has much greater impact.

Even though *teshuvah* is ultimately completed in the form of deed, it functionally begins with a realization or awakening. A person arrives, either suddenly or gradually, at a turning point in life. There is severe discomfort; a gnawing unease and anxiety takes hold, disturbing us out of the present. And whether or not we have faith in God, we are pressed to change—life can no longer move forward in the direction we have taken before. We see that we are flawed, and that if we are going to find peace of mind, something must be done. Once we have realized this, we can choose either to live freely by making an effort to change and amend our wrongdoings, or to remain in the numbing illusion of our lie—the lie that what we have done and who we are does not matter, that it is possible to live a divided, disingenuous life.

Functionally, *teshuvah* works through the following five steps:

• *Take a Moral Inventory.* We review and reflect upon our feelings of discontent, which might be in the form of fear, resentment, or shame. We honestly take stock of how those feelings may have been expressed in our behavior and affected our relationships with others (or even ourselves).

• *Confession.* We admit our part in whatever situation may have wronged someone in some way. This confession is ideally done with a trusted mentor, teacher, rabbi, or friend. One may also choose to journal the confession.

• *Prayerfully Intend to Right the Wrong.* We quietly observe the conflicting feelings and thoughts regarding the circumstance, asking God or a Greater Power for help in relieving oneself of the fear and guilt associated with the situation (forgiving oneself), as well as in mustering the courage and will to make it right.

• *Make Amends.* We address the injured party, apologizing for our part and asking what we might do, to whatever degree possible, to make it up to them.

• *Listen and Do.* Without judgment, we listen to the injured party and let ourselves take in and appreciate her or his experience of what occurred. We do not need to endure "abuse" or a "beating" in this response, as the point is to be humble and willing, without losing our personal dignity. If we are asked to do something reasonable, we promptly begin this process of reparation.

Teshuvah is not an annual event at the High Holidays but a daily one. We ask God to forgive us every single day in our daily, traditional prayer (the *Amidah*), referring to God as "The One Who Wants *Teshuvah*."[102] And since God wants *teshuvah* every day, we can assume that God expects us to make mistakes every day. We have daily confessionals in our prayers. (But they are not like the confessionals and absolutions of Catholicism; instead, we confess directly to God and to the person we have wronged.)

Undoubtedly, the process of *teshuvah* is not easy, but once we do it, we feel a sense of relief, freedom, and renewal. It takes a great deal of courage to both admit our imperfections and flaws, and then to face them with those we have wronged. It demands a collapse of pride, and often results in a change to a new identity. But it has been done time and again, and can be done in future when called for by me and by you. It allows us to either start our lives over, even at late stages in life, or to reenter previous lives with our family and community. Recognizing the magnitude of *teshuvah*, the Talmud stands in awe of those who sincerely go through its process, declaring: "Even the most righteous among us cannot stand in the place where one who has done *teshuvah* stands."[103]

Service—*Tikkun*

The great mystic Isaac Luria had a vision of time before time. In the beginning, he taught, there was no space, no time, no matter, only the energy and presence of God. But God felt divided and detached. God had the impulse to change, to grow, to create. In a way, God needed a helpmate.

Since there was only God, in order for God to create, God had to take a piece of God's own self to transform into matter and the universe. Therefore, God formed a vessel out of His own self in which to house the universe. This vessel would carry and grow God's energy toward unification and wholeness. Tragically, however, when God poured His energy into the vessel, the energy was too overwhelming and bright to be contained. The vessel shattered into pieces. But though the shards scattered, yet each remained attached to the emanation of energy and light that it had touched.

Thus, according to Jewish mystical cosmology, the universe that we all know to exist has been fundamentally broken since its point of beginning. Jewish spiritual teachers and later mystics have elaborated on the vision of the world as a broken cosmos—divinely shattered vessels attached to light—that still includes each and every part of the universe, including each of us who live in it. In other words, not only is the whole universe broken and divided but so is each one of us—broken shards affixed to and wrapped in light.

Hearkening to an earlier rabbinic concept—*tikkun olam* (literally, "repairing the world")—which generally signifies promoting the general welfare of the community,[104] Luria applied his concept of God and the universe, claiming that our purpose is to literally fix the world by putting the shattered vessel back together. In 1964, the chief rabbi of Israel, Abraham Isaac Kook, expanded Luria's concept when he wrote that *tikkun olam* must not be a process that "flies about solely in the spiritual ether" but instead must equitably bring together physical, social, and spiritual concerns.[105]

Tikkun olam, or *tikkun*, is ultimately the beautiful idea that we—as human beings—are a critical part of the unfolding of God's creation and will. When we balance ourselves through spiritual practice and then align our spiritual clarity with how we relate to others and the world, we can help to heal the brokenness. We see *tikkun* in our actions of service. We see it when we recognize the pain and brokenness in others, connect ourselves to them, and then serve their needs so they can become whole.

Sometimes our service comes in the form of providing for physical needs, such as food, clothes, shelter, or money. Sometimes our service is in the form of social or political needs, such as in advocacy, protest, or education. And sometimes our service is in the form of spiritual and emotional needs, such as listening, praying, sympathizing, and counseling.

Considering the mystical conception of a world created broken, with broken people, it is no wonder that such terrible things happen in it. That is simply the way the world was formed. But our purpose as a part of it is to find healing for ourselves and to provide healing for others.

Therefore, there is something we might learn from heartbreak: It does not—and for Judaism, must not—end in tragedy. In fact, heartbreak can lead to more openness, capaciousness, and power. The great sociologist and educator Parker Palmer describes this point succinctly:

> There are at least two ways to picture a broken *heart,* using heart in its original meaning not merely as the seat of the emotions but as the core of our sense of self. The conventional image, of course, is that of a heart broken by unbearable tension into a thousand shards—shards that sometimes become shrapnel aimed at the source of our pain. Every day, untold numbers of people try to "pick up the pieces," some of them taking grim satisfaction in the way the heart's explosion has injured their enemies. Here the broken heart is an unresolved wound that we too often inflict on others.

> But there is another way to visualize what a broken heart might mean. Imagine that small, clenched fist of a heart "broken open" into largeness of life, into greater capacity to hold one's own and

the world's pain and joy. This too happens every day. Who among us has not seen evidence, in our own or other people's lives, that compassion and grace can be the fruits of great suffering? Here heartbreak becomes a source of healing, enlarging our empathy and extending our ability to reach out.[106]

Jewish spiritual growth is the ultimate historical model of transforming curses into blessing. Rabbinic Judaism was born of tragedy, responding to the question of what to do with brokenness and a broken heart. After the Holocaust, the greatest tragedy in Jewish history is traditionally understood to be the destruction of the Second Temple in 70 C.E., when the Romans sacked and burned the center of Jewish life in Jerusalem. They destroyed not only the Holy Temple itself but also all that was attached to it, including the Jewish court of law (*Sanhedrin*), the marketplace beside it, and the heart of Jewish living and tradition. There were many questions as to how Judaism would survive without the Temple to worship in. How were Jews to serve God and atone for sins without the Temple and the offering of sacrifices? The sages were quick to respond in the following Talmudic passage, which is recited each morning in many traditional circles:

> Once, Rabban Yochanan ben Zakkai was walking with his disciple, Rabbi Yehoshua, near Jerusalem after the destruction of the Temple. Rabbi Yehoshua looked at the Temple ruins and said: "Alas for us! The place that atoned for the sins of the people of Israel—the ritual of animal sacrifice—lies in ruins!" Then Rabban Yochanan ben Zakkai spoke to him these words of comfort: "Be not grieved, my son. There is another equally meritorious way of gaining atonement even though the Temple is destroyed.

We can still gain atonement through deeds of compassion." For it is written, *Compassion I desire, not sacrifice* (Hosea, 6:6).[107]

Here we learn two significant lessons. One is the power of acts of compassion. These are the *tikkun* that we have been discussing. They are acts of service out of empathy and warmth without expectation of reward. Second, one of the critical reasons to offer sacrifices in the Temple was to atone for sins. Sacrificing a valuable animal actualized the abstract emotional and spiritual process that occurred inside the individual. When an individual saw his precious animal slaughtered and cooked, with smoke rising to the heavens, he believed and experienced the weight of his sins being lifted, and he could return to life with a clear conscience. Here we see that doing an act of goodness and healing for another can serve the same function. Many of us know this in our experience, i.e., doing something good for another person helps to ease the sting of our own pain—it lifts our spirits to know we have done something good and healing.

Communal Connection—*Kehilah*

The central narrative of the Jewish people is not of Abraham's awakening to monotheism. The central narrative of the Jewish people is one that involves the whole people—the narrative of community. Jewish peoplehood is defined by the shared story of all those who endured centuries of hardships and were liberated by a confluence of miraculous events. Then together, every single member of the community—young and old, rich and poor, men, women, children—stood together at Sinai and experienced the call of God. Since that moment, the Jewish people have been unified by a shared historical memory that informs our collective identity, ethics, and, ultimately, our destiny, hearkening to the Talmudic expression: "All of the people of Israel are responsible for one another."[108]

In today's world, there has been a loss of sense of community. This is the result of many complicated sociological and cultural factors, including the free market economy which allows families to be separated by states and even countries in search of job opportunities; suburbanization, which has widened people's distance from their community's core; the dissolution of the traditional neighborhood in many urban areas; and the dramatic consequences of secularization, which have further promoted the values of individualism and the breakdown of religious communal units. Of course, the advances of technology have certainly provided opportunities to connect in ways never previously experienced, but they have also simultaneously allowed many to remain isolated and sequestered from healthy human contact and relationships.

A contemporary conception reduces spirituality to the content of one's own heart alone. There are people who practice meditation, love and care for nature, champion the best practices of healthy living, and may even advocate on behalf of political and social justice—all incredible and praiseworthy. But their actions remain incomplete from the perspective of Jewish spirituality if these people are not engaged in their own community. As the sages declare: "Do not separate yourself from the community."[109]

Community is not always easy to engage. It is where we grow in our expression of respect, inclusion, responsibility, and justice. It is where we learn to appreciate the consequences of dishonesty, laziness, and resentment. The rabbinic sages understood well the value community offers in conversation. The Talmud, for example, contains thousands of unresolved arguments which each generation is left to figure out. We are compelled into conversation with one another, learning to argue, compromise, and agree with dignity, integrity, and continued loyalty. The democratic process of discussion, holding varying and conflicting perspectives while working through challenges, is where we learn to apply the values we study.

Community is messy and chaotic at times, but it is from that messy and chaotic place that creativity and moral fortitude blossom. Community is perhaps the most fertile ground for learning about ourselves and opportunities for growth. As poet and author Mark Nepo writes: "All things are connected. The art of community is discovering how."[110]

Furthermore, it is precisely because living in community is challenging and obliges us to respect one another's individuality that we learn how to belong. Living without the practice of engaging in a community can cause confusion about the difference between "fitting in" and belonging. More than we may realize, every one of us (especially our youths) is bombarded with claims in the media that to belong, we must "fit in." Look a certain way, we are told, wear the "right" clothes, join a certain organization, or get enough followers on Instagram and Snapchat. If we don't do that, we somehow are not "right" ourselves.

Rather than "fitting in," belonging is the need to feel as if we are connected to people and groups larger than ourselves. Belonging is incredibly important to healthy human development, with its foundational components of love, acceptance, and connection. Unfortunately, the pressure and coercion to "fit in" as the media describes it is usually shame-based—sending painful and damaging messages that the way we are is not worthy or "good enough." The difference between belonging and fitting in is this:

• *Belonging* is being somewhere you want to be, and where others want you.

• *Fitting in* is being where you want to be, but others there don't care one way or the other.

• *Belonging* is being accepted for "you."

• *Fitting in* is being accepted for being like everyone else.

• I get to be me if I *belong*. I have to be like you to *fit in*.[111]

Only by engaging in community do we truly learn and appreciate these distinctions, both in how they apply to us and how we apply them to others.

Finally, community functions as a team in the sense that it is where we learn our strengths and limitations. Only in community, when challenges are faced, do we learn where our strengths might best be applied.

There are times, though, when we realize we need help. Asking for help is also an important lesson. By asking for help, we grow in our connection with others, reinforcing the value of relational trust. Here we come to discover that our greatest strength may actually be the people around us—our community.

> A boy and his father were taking a hike in the hills. When they encountered a large rock blocking their path, the father said, "Go ahead, you can move it." The boy approached the rock and pushed, but to no avail. "I can't move it."
>
> "You can move it," the father said, "if you use all of your strength." The boy hunkered down and pressed as hard as he could using his back and legs. The rock hardly budged. "See, I used all of my strength, and I still couldn't move it."
>
> The father looked at his son and said gently, "No, you didn't use all of your strength. You didn't ask me for help."

Trust, respect, loyal responsibility, compromise for the sake of peace, and the humble willingness to help and be helped by others are the connective spiritual tissue that emerges in the midst of community. Sure, they can also be found in the workplace, the school, the market, but only through commitment to one's own community do we fully realize the power and beauty of these values in our personal and collective lives.

Exercise and Nutrition—*Shemirat Ha-Guf*

An old religious idea claims that the route to the divine is through the mind or spirit alone. But the unfortunate corollary has been to demean and denigrate the body. Consequently, the mind and spirit have come to represent what is good and noble, while the body is the seat of what is bad. In many religious circles, appetite, sex, and physical expression have come to represent temptation and immorality at worst, and nonsensical distractions at best.

Although this stream of thought can be found in the vast canon of Jewish spiritual and rabbinic literature, it is by no means the sole or authoritative stream. Largely and ultimately, Jewish spirituality is characterized by balance and harmony, as opposed to self-denial or asceticism.[112] The body and its needs (even its desires) is not something to be denied and repressed. It is an integrated vessel with which to sanctify our lives in service of the good. In turn, the body and mind and soul are understood to be partners in the spiritual experience, each with its own important level of consciousness; there is no inherent value judgment among body, mind, and soul, as the rabbis taught in this parable:

> The body and the soul can each free themselves from any harsh judgment. The body can say: "It is the soul who has sinned. Why, from the day it left me, I lie like a dumb stone in the grave!" And the soul can say: "It's the body who sinned. Why, from the day I left it, I fly about in the air like a bird without any sin!" . . . So, therefore, the Holy One, blessed be He, brings the soul and throws it into the body, and judges them together as one.[113]

Like the mind and spirit, the body also must be tended to[114] and appreciated and blessed each day.[115] After all, the body is literally what shapes our experience on this Earth and in this universe. It is the body through which we not only manifest our values and spirit but also learn some of our deepest lessons, such as our power to create, build, and heal through our hands; our caring love through intimacy and caress; and the beauty of the world through taste and sensation—as well as learning our power to hurt and destroy, and the devastation of pain and loss through decay and death.

Therefore, the body, and care for the body, is yet another portal toward spiritual growth. Bodily balance, the path to growth encouraged by Jewish spirituality, is most clearly represented in rabbinic literature regarding diet and nutrition. Certainly, many of us have heard of the Jewish dietary laws of *kashrut*, or kosher food (literally, "proper" or "fit" for consumption). Regrettably, the kosher rules and regulations are simply insufficient in today's world as guidance to maintaining one's health and fitness. They tell us what is permissible to eat and what is impermissible (e.g., pork, or mixing dairy and meat in the same meal) but with no mention of what is good or beneficial to eat.

But spiritual sages through the centuries have used their interpretations of the rationale for these kosher laws to deduce guiding philosophies for maintaining one's health. Chief among them is Maimonides, who was also a physician. Although countless dietary trends and fads have clearly come and gone, Maimonides' teachings of a balanced and disciplined diet, from nearly a millennium ago, would likely still hold up today as relevant and worthy of attention for health enthusiasts.[116]

Maimonides and other medieval sages essentially asserted that what our bodies consume influences both our physical and our spiritual well-being. Today nutritionists and researchers are corroborating this scientifically, showing that what we take within ourselves (both food and mind-altering substances like alcohol, drugs, and caffeine) can affect our emotions and cognitive functioning either favorably or adversely. Surely, those of us who strive to eat healthfully know the truth of these ideas through our own experience. And we can also see them manifested in organizational expressions across the globe through Jewish advocates for growing kosher organic food[117] and Jewish vegetarianism.[118]

Physical hygiene and exercise, although not emphasized nearly enough in rabbinic literature (possibly because of historical circumstances), is also a value, as proper balance of vigorous activity with sleep and relaxation is essential to spiritual living.[119] Indeed, many of us might consider exercise and hygiene as central to our spiritual and mental well-being, since we feel less alive and energized when we go without them. We need to simply look at the racks of popular magazines and scientific journals to understand the cross-cultural, international acceptance of the healing effect— physically, psychologically, and spiritually—of taking care of the body through proper exercise and nutrition. Spiritual growth happens through the process of integrating all parts of ourselves: mind, soul, *and body*.

Recreation—*Hit'chadshut*

It has been said that everyone needs something to look forward to. This does not mean restless anticipation of some future unknown or desire for a fleeting escape from the present. Looking forward in this sense is actually an expression of the acceptance of reality as it is. The reality is that among the things we need to have balanced in our lives is the cycles of time. For many of us, the week is spent largely doing some form of work: jobs, chores, weekly bills, general *schlepping* from place to place. Even if we take all our spiritual practices seriously and live as mindfully as we can from day to day and week to week, we still may end up with imbalance of energy in our budget. Over time, this can mount up, weighing heavily on us. Looking forward to something is a way to build in opportunities to refresh and reinvigorate ourselves.

The Jewish concept of Shabbat—the spiritual institution of the Sabbath—is a sacred time we can look forward to as an opportunity to rejuvenate and renew. Shabbat is fundamentally a day to pause and allow ourselves to be free from the circumstances and conditions of life; it is a day built into our consciousness as part of the fabric of time that safeguards our well-being and spiritual health. Shabbat is a day each week to, as one synagogue puts it, "power down."[120] It is a day for relieving ourselves from the burdens of daily life and returning to a spiritually (and socially) level ground where are no titles to uphold, no money to budget, no deadlines to manage, and no next place to be. Shabbat is a release from external demands and expectations, and by being free of them, an opportunity to become whole again. It is when we reconstitute our wholeness, when we "re-member" both individually and as a community ("re-member," as in the opposite of "dis-member"). In this way, Shabbat is surely the holiest day of the week, and perhaps the holiest day of the year.

According to Jewish spiritual time, Shabbat is the day around which the entire week revolves. In the Jewish tradition, as well as the Hebrew language, each day of the week is identified by its relationship to Shabbat, i.e., Sunday is *Yom Rishon shel Shabbat*, which means, "First Day in accord with Shabbat," and so on through Friday, *Yom Shishi shel Shabbat*, "Sixth Day in accord with Shabbat." From the Jewish tradition's perspective, we are always in a spiritually temporal relationship with Shabbat. In other words, each day we are literally counting toward Shabbat; we are literally always looking forward to our day of relief and freedom.

But despite the aptness of seeing Shabbat as a day to "power down," the truth is that as a time of relief, freedom, and separation from the mundane, it also is a day we "power up." The discipline of will power, energy, and attention that we use to adhere to schedules and generally get things done has only a certain amount of "battery life" before it needs to be recharged. This is required not because of a depletion of our mental strength[121] but rather by a need for spiritual renewal and inspiration, which is fueled by a shift in perspective. Mordecai Kaplan, the great thinker and teacher, famously described that value of Shabbat as such a renewal of vision:

> An artist cannot be continually wielding his or her
> brush. The painter must stop painting at times to
> freshen his or her vision of the object, the meaning
> of which the artist wishes to express on canvas. The
> Shabbat represents those moments when we pause in
> our brushwork to renew our vision of the general
> plan. Having done so, we take ourselves to our
> painting with clarified vision and renewed energy.[122]

Shabbat, as Kaplan describes, is really a paradigm for what we need even more than Shabbat itself. Rather than terms like "renewal" or "renewed energy," Shabbat affords us the experience of "re-creation," or being "re-created." After all, that is the axiomatic principle for what Shabbat represents (the creation of the world). Yes, we need it on Shabbat but also in other ways; we need "Shabbat plus."

Certainly, other holidays as well as birthdays and family celebrations can provide a taste of Shabbat. But we also each need to look forward to our own individual paths to re-creation and renewal. For some of us, that may mean camping, hiking, traveling abroad, or even something adventurous or athletic like skydiving or windsurfing. Planning these kinds of trips and events gives us memorable moments to look forward to; this is our life, and living big, broad adventures and stories brings meaning to our time here.

Naturally, the big events are not always possible because of scheduling, money, or circumstance. So we need smaller, weekly opportunities for relief and fun to look forward to. It might be going to a favorite ice cream shop for the flavor of the month, meeting a friend at a popular sushi restaurant, indulging in that movie we can't wait to see. Or it might simply mean taking a few extra, undisturbed morning hours in bed to read a good book with coffee.

Recreation is renewal, it is self-care (which is not the same as being selfish), it is old-fashioned fun, and it is a part of the necessary healing in our lives. We are here to be responsible and grow, and yet, paradoxically, we cannot do so unless we take care of ourselves and appreciate the tastes and beauty of the world, our home. The Jewish tradition teaches us to enjoy the marvels of our life and the world, for anything else is an affront to God as the Creator of this life and the world's wonders.

Reference Notes

Introduction
[1] Jaruwan Sakulku, "The Impostor Phenomenon." *International Journal of Behavioral Science.* 6:1 (2011): 73–92; Carl Richards, "Learning to Deal With the Impostor Syndrome," *The New York Times*, (October 26, 2015); Pauline Rose Clance & Suzanne Ament Imes, "The imposter phenomenon in high achieving women: dynamics and therapeutic intervention." *Psychotherapy: Theory, Research & Practice* (Fall, 1978).

[2] See the book by Rabbi Jack Bloom, *The Rabbi as Symbolic Exemplar* (NY: Routledge Press, 2002).

[3] Psalms 130:1-2.

1. A Vision of Spiritual Growth
[4] See Rashi on Genesis 1:1.

[5] Sandra Blakeslee, "Tracing the Brain's Pathways for Linking Emotion, Reason," *The New York Times*, (Dec., 6,1994). http://www.nytimes.com/1994/12/06/science/tracing-the-brain-s-pathways-for-linking-emotion-and-reason.html?pagewanted=all; "Decisions and Desire," Gardiner Morse (Jan. 2006, Harvard Business Review). https://hbr.org/2006/01/decisions-and-desire.

[6] Lindberg, S.M., Hyde, J.S., Peterson, J.L, & Linn, M.C., "New trends in gender and mathematics performance: a meta-analysis," *Psychol Bull.* 136:6 (2010): 1123–1135; Hyde, J.S., Mertz, J.E., "Gender, culture, and mathematics performance, *Proceedings of the National Academy of Sciences*, 106:22, (2009): 8801-8807.

[7] I am grateful to Rabbi Bradley Shavit Artson for his lecture on the interpretation of the trees in the Garden of Eden which served as a resource and inspiration for several parts of this chapter.

[8] Rabbeinu Bachya, on Genesis 2:9, wrote that the Tree of Knowledge and the Tree of Life were both in the center of the Garden, for they formed one tree at the bottom, and branched into two when they reached a certain height.

[9] It is worth noting here that when Adam and Eve ate from the tree, they did not sin. "Sin" is a word that carries too much weight for what they did. Sin connotes an attribute of everlasting spiritual stain, which cannot be cleansed. The category of sin of which one cannot repent and transform in Jewish spirituality is actually a very narrow one to which the likes of only few would apply. Sin is a label, a scarlet letter that forever defines a person. Sin is not of Jewish spirituality. The word for sin in Hebrew is *chet*, which is derived from an archery term, meaning, "missing the mark." The difference is astounding. "Missing the mark" is an action which can be corrected; sin is a state of being that remains. Adam and Eve missed the mark; we miss the mark, which means that we can do better the next opportunity. Sin must be redefined as a mistake, which we can be corrected, a lie that we tell ourselves or an act of disrespect for which can be forgiven. Adam and Eve ate from the fruit, broke the rule, something that any one of us could easily do. Yet such a deviation from truth cannot and should not prevent them or anyone else rom correcting it. That can only happen, however, through self-reflection, learning, and trying again.

[10] The Torah is consistently referred to as the Tree of Life, *Etz Chayim* both in liturgy and rabbinic literature. Kabbalistic literature often refers to the Tree of Life as simultaneously both the Torah and the spiritual composition of God. When referencing God's manner of expression alone, the Tree of Life is synonymously referred to as the *Sefirot*, or spheres of God's expression.

[11] Mishnah, *Avot* 5:25.

2. Acknowledging Brokenness

[12] *The Tanya: Bi-Lingual Edition*. Trans. Nissim Mindel (NY: Kehot Publication Society, 1998), p. 1.

[13] See Martin Buber, *Ten Rungs: Collected Hasidic Sayings* (NY: Schocken Press, 1947; reprint 1995 Citadel Press), p. 65. This adapted version of this teaching can also be found in Parker Palmer's *The Politics of the Brokenhearted* (Kalamazoo, MI: Fetzer Institute, 2005), p. 232. Accessed online at www.fetzer.org/sites/default/files/images/resources/attachment/2012-07-12/dad_palmer_essay.pdf.

[14] See Mishnah, *Avot* 4:29, where it says: "It was not your will that formed you, nor was it your will that gave you birth; it is not your will that makes you live, and it is not your will that brings you death."

[15] See Mishnah, *Avot* 2:4: "Do God's will as though it were yours, so that God will do your will as though it were God's."

[16] *Katha Upanishad*, 2.2.14, 15; *Mundaka Upanishad*, 3.2.1, 2. Translation from Nicholas Lash, *The Beginning and End of Religion* (NY: Cambridge University Press, 1996), p. 34.

[17] The "deeply spiritual way" refers to Buddhism's Eightfold Noble Path of right perspective, intention, speech, action, livelihood, effort, mindfulness, and concentration. For an exact translation of the Four Noble Truths *see* Bhikkhu Bodhi, trans., *Dhammacak- kapavattana Sutta: Samyutta Nikaya LVI, 11*, "Setting in Motion the Wheel of the Dhamma," http://www.budsas.org/ebud/ebsut001.htm.

[18] John 2:15-17.

[19] Eccles. 2:10-11.

[20] Tillich used the term "ultimate concern." See Paul Tillich, *Dynamics of Faith* (New York: Harper & Row, 1957), p. 1. Heschel used the term "ultimacy." See Abraham Joshua Heschel, *God in Search of Man* (New York: Farrar, Straus, and Giroux, 1955), p. 125.

[21] Deut. 6:4–5. The interpretive, Rabbinic tradition represents the general understanding of what it means to love God with heart, soul, and might. Accordingly, the Rabbis teach that loving God with one's heart means to turn over our impulses and selfish desires to the love of God (Mishnah, *Berakhot* 9:5). Loving God with all of one's soul is to turn over our very lives to God, as exemplified by Rabbi Akiva in the first century. See B.T., *Berakhot* 61b. And loving God with one's might means turning over our desire for bodily and material wealth. *Sifrei Devarim*; see also Rashi on Deut. 6:5.

[22] *Guide for the Perplexed* 1:36.

[23] *Sefer Ha-Chinukh*, 429

[24] *Tanya*, p. 93. The Talmud (*Sotah* 4b) expresses a similar concept, stating, "Every person that is arrogant (*gasut ha-ru'ach*), it is as though they worship idols."

[25] *S'fat Emet* 2:40, Translation adapted from Arthur Green, *The Language of Truth: The Torah Commentary of the Sefat Emet, Rabbi Yehudah Aryeh Leib Alter of Ger* (Philadelphia: JPS, 1998), p. 90.

[26] Nachmanides on Exod. 6:9.

[27] *Sefer Mitzvot Ha-Gadol*, Introduction to Positive Commandments. Translation from *High Holiday Prayer Book*, compiled and arranged by Rabbi Morris Silverman (Bridgeport, Conn.: Prayer Book Press, 1951), p. 443.

3. Awakening to Our Story

[28]   *Sefer Yetzirah* 1:1, "God created His universe with three books (*s'farim*): with text (*sefer*), with number (*s'far*), and storytelling (*sippur*)."

[29]   *Targum Onkelos* on Genesis 2:7.

[30]   Gregory Bateson, *Mind and Nature: A Necessary Unity* (New York: Bantam Books, 1979), p. 14.

[31]   *Likkutei Halakhot, Nedarim* 5:6-8; translation from the *Breslov Haggadah*, compiled by Yehoshua Starret (Jerusalem: Breslov Research Institute, 1989), p. 37-38.

[32]   See Mishnah, *Avot* 2:5, as Hillel said, "Do not judge someone until you have put yourself in his place."

[33]   For one example, see https://www.rte.ie/lifestyle/living/2016/0914/816490-speed-yoga-for-shorter-mornings/.

[34]   Joseph Campbell, *The Power of Myth* (New York: Doubleday, 1988), p. 3-4.

[35]   Bilaam's donkey in Numbers 22:28-30.

[36]   This story has appeared in many adapted forms and its original author is unknown. Occasionally referred to as "The Rabbi's Gift," a version of the story appears in the book, *The Different Drum: Community Making and Peace, by M. Scott Peck* (New York: Simon & Schuster, 1987), p. 13-15.

[37]   *The Power of Myth*, p. 120.

[38]   Martin Buber, *Ten Rungs: Collected Hasidic Sayings* (NY: Schocken Press, 1947; reprint 1995 Citadel Press), p. 73.

4. Facing Our Counterpart

[39]   The phrase "and God saw that it was good"—*va-yar Elohim ki tov*—is the repeating refrain after the days of creation in Genesis 1. See verses 1:4, 10, 12, 18, 21, 25, and 31. It is noteworthy, however, that this phrase does not occur after the second day of creation (of which there is a great deal of commentary) and it is twice repeated on the third and sixth days.

[40]   Martin Buber, *Ten Rungs: Collected Hasidic Sayings* (NY: Schocken Press, 1947; reprint 1995 Citadel Press), p. 20.

[41]   Genesis 2:18.

[42]   The US Department of Health and Human Services states, "by age 40, approximately 87% of non-offending men were married compared with only 40% of men with a history of incarceration." See, https://aspe.hhs.gov/legacy-page/incarceration-family-review-research-promising-approaches-serving-fathers-families-effects-incarceration-intimate-partner-relationships-

146366#TOC.

[43] Midrash, *Bereishit Rabbah* 17:6.

[44] Genesis 1:27.

[45] Midrash, *Bereishit Rabbah* 8:1. There are similar themes in Plato's *Symposium* and other ancient traditions; see the references by Louis Ginzberg, *Legends of the Jews*, vol. 5, (Philadelphia: JPS, 1925), pp. 88-89, n. 42.

[46] Genesis 2:18. "Fitting helper for him" is the translation of *ezer k'negdo* used by the Jewish Publication Society. Translations vary for the term, including "helper suitable for him," "helper who is just right for him," "help meet for him," helper fit for him," "helper comparable to him," "a helper that is his counterpart" and "a companion for him who corresponds to him." It is interesting to note that the numerical equivalent (*gematriyah*) of *ezer k'negdo* is 360. Of course, 360 degrees make a complete circle, representing wholeness and, incidentally, comprising the shape of the wedding ring.

[47] The statement, "We are not human beings having a spiritual experience; we are spiritual beings having a human experience," has been widely used and most commonly attributed to Pierre Teilhard de Chardin, an early twentieth century French paleontologist and Jesuit priest.

[48] Buber, *Ten Rungs*, p. 89-90.

[49] See Genesis 3:20.

5. The Struggle: Living as Israel

[50] Rabbi Joseph B. Soloveitchik, "Sacred and Profane: *Kodesh* and *Hol* in World Perspectives," *Gesher*, 2, no. 1 (1966): 7. The word "holiness" in the quotation is my translation of the Hebrew *kedushah*, which is what appears in the original article. *Kedushah* is alternatively translated as "sacred."

[51] Genesis 25:22.

[52] Genesis 25:26.

[53] Genesis 25:27.

[54] Genesis 28:12.

[55] The Talmud (*Chullin* 91a), suggests that he particularly went back to get some small jars. Some later Rabbinic authorities would say that these were jars of oil, the very same oil which miraculously burned during the rededication of the Temple celebrated at Hanukkah.

[56] Genesis 32:25.

[57] Genesis 32:31. Also, according to the prophet Hosea's account (Hos. 12:4), the man is identified as an angel.

58   Midrash, *Bereishit Rabbah* 77:3.

59   Note tha *va-yivater* in chapter 32 is spelled with a *vav* and with a *vet* in chapter 15 of Genesis. This slight written difference of the word, however, does not diminish the literary connection. Since the words sound so similar the listener to the Torah would be able to make this natural association, especially since these are the only occurrences of the word.

60   Erich Fromm, *Man For Himself* (New York. Holt, Rinehart, and Winston, 1947), p. 20.

61   "Esteemable acts" is a commonly used phrase in 12 Step programs and fellowships as a path toward personal transformation.

62   B. Talmud, *Sanhedrin* 37a.

63   *Sefer Mitzvot Ha-Gadol*, Introduction to the Positive Commandments.

64   Mishnah, *Avot* 4:1.

6. The Way of Balance

65   *Hineini*, literally, "Here I am," is an expression used several times in the Torah in order to convey one being fully attentive and present. It emblematically appears in the story of the Binding of Isaac (*Akeidat Yitzchak*) found in Genesis, chapter 22.

66   Aryeh Kaplan, *Inner Space* (Jerusalem: Moznaim Press, 1991), p. 63.

67   Alan Morinis, *Everyday Holiness: The Jewish Spiritual Path of Mussar* (Boston: Trumpeter Books, 2007), p. 20.

68   Ira F. Stone, *A Responsible Life, The Spiritual Path of Mussar* (NY: Aviv Press, 2006), p. xxi.

69   *Pirkei Avot: Shemoneh Perakim of the Rambam*; trans. Rabbi Eliyahu Touger (NY: Moznaim Press, 1994), pp. 24-5.

70   "Jewish Ethics" in *Encyclopedia of Ethics*, eds. Lawrence C. Becker & Charlotte B. Becker (NY: Routledge Press, 2001), pg. 913. Aristotle describes ethical virtues as intermediate dispositions or conditions between two states: excess and deficiency. He suggests that in order to avoid either the excess or the deficiency, one must judge wisely between what the circumstance and condition calls for.

71   See *The Autobiography of Benjamin Franklin*, especially pp. 38-42 at http://www.ushistory.org/franklin/autobiography/page38.htm

72   *See* Jewish Women's Archive. ""Merger Poem Poster" by Judy Chicago,

1988." (Viewed on April 13, 2018) <https://jwa.org/media/chicago-judy-1-still-image>

[73] Aryeh Kaplan, *Jewish Meditation: A Practical Guide* (NY: Schocken Books, 1985), p. 4.

[74] "Acceptance was the answer." *Alcoholics Anonymous, 4th ed.* (NY: A.A. World Service, 2001), pp. 417,420.

[75] Abraham Joshua Heschel, *God in Search of Man* (NY: Farrar, Strauss, and Giroux, 1955), pp. 136-137; Arthur Green, "God's need for man: a unitive approach to the writings of Abraham Joshua Heschel" *Modern Judaism: A Journal of Jewish Ideas and Experience*, v. 35:1, (2015): 247–261.

7. Welcoming in Joy

[76] Abraham Joshua Heschel, *A Passion for Truth* (Woodstock, VT: Jewish Lights, 2004 rpt.), p. 52. This quote is referring to the Hasidic perspective of joy, as it was taught by the Baal Shem Tov. The quotations are referring to the final traditional blessing recited at a wedding, which refers to God as the "one who created delight and joy," *asher bara sason v'simchah.*

[77] B. Talmud, *Ta'anit* 29a: "When the month of Adar [during which Purim occurs] joy is increased."

[78] Psalm 30:4, 6.

[79] "Anatomy of Gratitude," transcript of interview (Dec. 17, 2017) for *On Being.* https://onbeing.org/programs/david-steindl-rast-anatomy-of-gratitude-dec2017/

[80] "The Pursuit of Joy (Ki Tavo 5775)" from *Covenant and Conversation.* http://rabbisacks.org/the-pursuit-of-joy-ki-tavo-5775/

[81] Viktor Frankl, *Man's Search for Meaning*, 4th ed. (Boston, MA: Beacon Press, 1992), p. 143.

[82] Brené Brown, *The Gifts of Imperfection* (Center City, Minn: Hazelden, 2010), p. 81.

[83] It is understood that the phrase "waiting for the other shoe to drop" was born in the New York tenements in the early 1900s, in which many Jewish immigrants lived. The tenements were built similar in design with the bedrooms directly atop one another. Therefore, it was normal to hear a neighbor above removing his or her shoes one at a time. As the first shoe made a sound hitting, the expectation was to hear or expect the next shoe to drop at any moment.

[84] David Wolpe, "From Suffering, Compassion," *The Jewish Week* (6-5-14):

http://www.thejewishweek.com/editorial-opinion/musings/suffering-compassion

85 *Sifre*, Deuteronomy, 41 (to 11:13).

86 Abraham Joshua Heschel, *God in Search of Man*. NY: Farrar, Strauss, and Giroux, 1955), p. 385.

87 See B. Talmud, *Berakhot* 62a-b, wherein a disciple follows his master to the outhouse and the bedroom to learn Torah from him.

88 Anne Lamott, *Plan B: Further Thoughts on Faith* (NY: Riverhead Books, 2005), p. 66.

89 Known as *Sayver Panim Yafot*; see Mishnah, *Avot* 1:15.

90 Abraham Joshua Heschel, *A Passion for Truth* (Woodstock, VT: Jewish Lights, 2004 rpt.), p. 52.

91 Nathan Ausubel, *A Treasury of Jewish Folklore* (NY: Crown, 1948), p. 264.

92 Stan Pollack, *The Golden Age of Tongue Kissing: Brooklyn 23, NY* (NY: Xlibiris, 2002), p. 54.

93 B. Talmud, *Ta'anit* 22a.

8. A Suggested Program for Spiritual Growth

94 *Tiferet Shlomo* (Rabbi Shlomo Rabinowich of Radomsk, 1803-1866, Poland), *Parshat Chukat*.

95 See also Maimonides, *Shemonah Perakim*.

96 *S'fat Emet* 1:60, Translation adapted from Arthur Green, *The Language of Truth: The Torah Commentary of the Sefat Emet, Rabbi Yehudah Aryeh Leib Alter of Ger* (Philadelphia: JPS, 1998), p. 22.

97 Arriving at this notion of a desired result for spiritual growth came after a long period of study and reflection. After reading many books and passages from scholars and sages, including biographies and sketches of successful living, a phrase jumped out from the Hall of Fame basketball coach John Wooden's book on how he developed his incredible and nuanced "Pyramid of Success." See *Wooden on Leadership* by John Wooden and Steve Jamison (NY: McGraw Hill, 2005). His Pyramid succinctly flows from his clear definition of success, which states: "Success is peace of mind, which is a direct result of self-satisfaction in knowing you made the effort to do your best to become the best that you are capable of becoming." The simplicity of the definition and its remarkably personal and qualitative, rather than quantitative character is striking. It is as much spiritual as it is practical. The open-

ing words, however, resounded as a quintessential spiritual statement and has stuck with this author ever since.

[98] Miller, G.A., The magical number seven, plus or minus two: Some limits on our capacity for processing information. Psychological Review. 63:2, (1956): 81-97

[99] While Rabbi Schulweis, z"l, actually said this to me directly, he has written something similar in his poem "Fear of Death": "Fear—not of death or dying but of not having lived." This poem can be found in Harold Schulweis, *Finding Each Other in Judaism: Meditations on the Rites of Passage from Birth to Immortality* (NY: UAHC Press, 2001), p. 92.

[100] Mishnah, *Avot* 1:14.

[101] From 1972 interview with Carl Stern on the NBC broadcast "Eternal Light." See interview transcript http://www.philosophy-religion.org/religion_links/aj_heschel.htm.

[102] The theme of the fifth prayer of the thrice-daily recited *Amidah* prayer is *teshuvah*. The prayer reads: "Return us our Father to Your Torah, bring us close to Your service and influence us to make a complete *teshuvah* before You. Blessed are You, God, the One who Wants *Teshuvah*."

[103] B. Talmud, *Berakhot* 34b.

[104] See Mishnah, *Gittin* 4:2.

[105] Kook, Abraham Isaac. *Orot Ha-Kodesh*, sect. 3, pg. 180.

[106] Parker Palmer, *The Politics of the Brokenhearted* (Kalamazoo, MI: Fetzer Institute, 2005), p. 232.

[107] *Avot de Rabbi Natan* 4:5.

[108] B. Talmud, *Shevuot* 39a.

[109] Mishnah, *Avot* 2:5.

[110] Mark Nepo, "Unfinished Painting." Parabola Magazine (2016). https://parabola.org/2016/01/18/unfinished-painting/

[111] See Brené Brown, *The Gifts of Imperfection*. Center City, Minn: Hazelden, 2010), pp. 23-30.

[112] Abraham Joshua Heschel (NY: Farrar, Strauss, and Giroux, 1951), *Man is Not Alone*, p. 263

[113] B. Talmud, *Sanhedrin* 91b.

[114] See Midrash, *Leviticus Rabbah* 34:3: *The loving man rewards himself* [Proverbs 11:17]. This refers to Hillel the Elder who, when he took leave of

his students, used to walk with them a little way. His students asked him, "Rabbi, where are you walking to?" He answered, "To do a mitzvah." They asked, "What mitzvah?" He replied, "To take a bath in the bathhouse." They said to him, "Is that really a mitzvah?" He replied, "Certainly! If the statues erected to kings in the theaters and circuses are washed and scrubbed by those in charge of them. . .how much more should I, who have been created in God's image and likeness, [wash and scrub my body], as it is written *For in the image of God he made man* [Genesis 9:6]." Another version of this story runs. . ."Rabbi, where are you going to?" To which he replied, "To do a charitable deed for a guest in my house." They asked him, "Does this guest stay with you every day?" He answered, "This poor soul—is it not a guest in the body? It is here today and gone tomorrow!"

[115] Jewish tradition includes a daily morning blessing for the body, which says: "Praised are You, Lord our God King of the universe, who with wisdom fashioned the human body, creating openings, arteries, glands and organs, marvelous in structure, intricate in design. Should but one of them, by being blocked or opened, fail to function, it would be impossible to exist. Praised are You, Lord, healer of all flesh who sustains our bodies in wondrous ways."

[116] See Maimonides, *Mishneh Torah,* The Laws of Proper Behavior, 3:2-3.

[117] E.g., Urban Adamah: https://urbanadamah.org/

[118] See https://www.jewishveg.org/torah.html

[119] Maimonides, *Mishneh Torah,* The Laws of Proper Behavior, 4:15; *Avodat Ha-Kodesh, Moreh b'Etzba* 3-123, as quoted by Yitzchak Buxbaum in *Jewish Spiritual Practices,* p. 654.

[120] Upon attending a Shabbat service at Ikar in Los Angeles, I noticed the signs and Shabbat bulletin used that expression to capture the spirit of Shabbat in this technologically immersed world.

[121] "New research challenges the idea that willpower is a limited resource." *British Psychological Society Research Digest* (June 24, 2015): https://digest.bps.org.uk/2015/06/24/new-research-challenges-the-idea-that-willpower-is-a-limited-resource/

[122] Mordecai Kaplan, *The Meaning of God* (Detroit: Wayne St. University Press, 1937, rpt. 1994) p. 59

Glossary

Baal Shem Tov (1698-1760, Ukraine). Yisrael ben Eliezer, known as the Baal Shem Tov ("Master of the Good Name"), is understood to be the founder of Hasidism. Most of the biographical information about him is in the form of stories and legends passed on by his disciples. They describe the Baal Shem Tov (also referred to by the acronym *Besht*) as coming from a poor and simple family. His special abilities relating to mysticism began at an early age, and legend claims that he worked miracles and battled demons. His teachings emphasize the spiritual through joy in living and the power and transcendence of prayer.

Gemara. Usually referred to as the Talmud, though this is technically erroneous. The Gemara (literally, "Completion") is the discussion of and commentary on the laws of the Mishnah by the rabbinic sages of the second through fifth centuries C.E.

Heschel, Abraham Joshua. One of the great and most widely quoted Jewish religious philosophers of the modern era (1907-1972, Poland, Germany, USA). Born into a Hasidic family, he studied Talmud in Germany, and after escaping the Nazis, taught at Hebrew Union College and Jewish Theological Seminary. He is also known for being extremely active in both the civil rights and the Jewish-Christian interfaith movements. His most famous books are his theological ones, including *The Sabbath, God in Search of Man*, and *Man Is Not Alone*.

Kabbalah (literally, "Reception"). The tradition of Jewish mysticism which maintains that there are hidden truths within the

Torah. The primary resource for Kabbalah is the Zohar. Hasidism is based on many of the teachings of Kabbalah.

Kaplan, Aryeh. An American Orthodox rabbi and author, known for his prolific teachings on Jewish mysticism and philosophy (1934-1983). His most popular books are *The Living Torah, Innerspace,* and *Jewish Meditation.*

Kaplan, Mordecai (1881-1983, Lithuania and USA). A highly influential and controversial rabbi in the Conservative stream of Judaism. He founded the Teachers Institute in 1909 at the Jewish Theological Seminary and would later develop a philosophy that led to the Reconstructionist movement, which has established many modern Jewish institutions. Kaplan's theology held that in light of advances in philosophy, science, and history, it would be impossible for modern Jews to continue to adhere to many of Judaism's traditional theological claims. Among his works are *Judaism as a Civilization* and *The Meaning of God in Modern Jewish Religion.*

kavanah (literally, "intention"). The mental and spiritual attention and association a person applies to one's rituals or practices. This is as opposed to ritual or practice done solely by rote or routine.

Maimonides/Rambam. Rabbi Moses ben Maimon (1135–1204; Spain and Egypt), a physician and possibly the greatest Jewish thinker of all time. He wrote many important works, including legal codes and philosophical expositions. Among them are the *Mishneh Torah,* the first written Jewish legal code, which is written in remarkably clear Hebrew, and the *Guide for the Perplexed,* a work tremendously influenced by Aristotelian philosophy which interprets the Torah with the objective of eliminating apparent contradictions with philosophy.

Midrash (literally, "Elucidation" or "Exposition"). A body of work that combines the theological, homiletical, and ethical lore of the Palestinian rabbis from the third through tenth centuries C.E.

Mishnah (literally, "Teaching"). The first compilation of the Oral Law and the foundational text for the Talmud and the rabbinic tradition.

mitzvah (literally, "commandment"); pl. ***mitzvot.*** One of the religious obligations detailed in the Torah, most of which fall into the positive category of religious, ethical, or moral obligations. The Torah also contains negative mitzvot, which are prohibitions. When a boy has his Bar Mitzvah or a girl her Bat Mitzvah, they become, respectively, a "son" or "daughter" of the commandment—meaning a full-fledged member of the Jewish community now assuming the responsibilities of Jewish law.

Rabbinic Tradition. Following the destruction of the Second Temple and the Jewish Court (the *Sanhedrin*) in 70 C.E., the centralization of Jewish thought and expression became embodied within the rabbis of the Jewish tradition. Though this tradition is best captured in the legal and moral expositions of the classical Talmud and Midrash, the process of interpretation continues to this day. The rabbinic tradition is characterized by a relentless willingness to question the Bible and analyze the works of previous generations of scholars and rabbis. More than the Hebrew Bible, Judaism is an outgrowth of the interpretation, commentary, legal responsa, and teachings of the rabbis across the millennia.

Talmud. The central and most important body of rabbinic literature. Combining the Mishnah and Gemara, the Talmud contains material from rabbinic academies dating from before the second through the sixth century C.E. In its sixty-three areas of study, it includes learned expositions, wisdom, personal stories, and arguments. There are two versions: the more-extensive Babylonian (*Bavli*) Talmud, which is generally what is being referred to, and the Jerusalem (*Yerushalmi*), or Palestinian Talmud. The Talmud serves as the primary source for all later codes of Jewish law.

Tanakh. This is what Jews are referring to when they speak of the Bible. Tanakh is an acronym for the three books that make up the cornerstone of Jewish beliefs: the Torah (the Five Books of Moses), Nevi'im (Prophets), and Ketuvim (Writings).

Zohar (literally, "Illumination"). A book of mystical commentaries on the Tanakh that mixes together theology, psychology, myth, ancient Gnosticism, and superstition. The objective is to uncover the deepest mysteries of the world, namely why God created the universe, how God is manifest in the world, and what the forces of life are.

Suggested Reading

Anonymous. *Alcoholics Anonymous, 4th ed.* New York: A.A. World Services, Inc., 2001.

Borowitz, E. & Weinman Schwartz, F. *The Jewish Moral Virtues.* Philadelphia: Jewish Publication Society, 1999.

Brown, Brené. *The Gifts of Imperfection.* Center City, MN: Hazelden, 2010.

Buber, Martin. *Ten Rungs: Collected Hasidic Sayings.* London, Routledge Press, 1947.

Heschel, Abraham Joshua. *God in Search of Man.* New York, Farrar, Straus, Giroux, 1955.

Heschel, Abraham Joshua. *A Passion for Truth.* Woodstock, VT: Jewish Lights, 2004 rpt.

Frankel, Estelle. *The Wisdom of Not Knowing.* Boulder, CO: Shambhala, 2017.

Frankl, Viktor. *Man's Search for Meaning.* Boston: Beacon Press, 2006.

Fromm, Erich. *Man For Himself.* New York. Holt, Rinehart, and Winston, 1947.

Kaplan, Aryeh. *Inner Space.* Jerusalem: Moznaim Press, 1991.

Kaplan, Mordecai. *Questions Jews Ask: Reconstructionist Answers.* New York: Reconstructionist Press, 1956.

Levy, Naomi. *Talking to God: Personal Prayers for Times of Joy, Sadness, Struggle, and Celebration.* New York: Random House, 2002.

Luzzatto, Moshe Chaim. (trans. Aryeh Kaplan). *The Way of God.* New York, Feldheim Publishers, 1997.

Miller, Lisa. *The Spiritual Child.* New York: St. Martin's Press, 2015.

Morinis, Alan. *Everyday Holiness.* Boston: Trumpeter Books, 2007.

Newman, Louis I (ed.). *The Hasidic Anthology.* Northvale, N.J.: Jason Aronson, 1963.

Shapiro, Rami. *Tanya, the Masterpiece of Hasidic Wisdom.* Woodstock, VT: Skylights Publishing, 2010.

Steinberg, Paul. *Recovery, the 12 Steps, and Jewish Spirituality.* Woodstock, VT: Jewish Lights, 2014.

Steinberg, Paul, *Celebrating the Jewish Year, Volumes 1–3.* Philadelphia: Jewish Publication Society, 2007 & 2009.

Stone, Ira F. *A Responsible Life: The Spiritual Path of Mussar.* NY: Aviv Press, 2006.

About the Author

Rabbi Paul Steinberg is a nationally recognized transformative educator and speaker on spirituality.

He is currently serving at Congregation Kol Shofar in Tiburon, California, and previously was Community Rabbi and Spiritual Adviser at the acclaimed Beit T'Shuvah synagogue community and addiction treatment center in Los Angeles.

He has published many articles on Jewish thought and education, as well as five books: *Study Guide to Jewish Ethics;* the three-volume *Celebrating the Jewish Year*—which won the National Jewish Book Award; and *Recovery, the 12 Steps and Jewish Spirituality: Reclaiming Hope, Courage & Wholeness*— the first comprehensive approach to integrating Jewish spirituality with the principles of the 12-Step programs. He is a nationally noted speaker and consultant regarding issues of mental health and addiction in the Jewish community.

Rabbi Steinberg began his career as the Director of Jewish Studies and Hebrew at Levine Academy in Dallas, and went on to become Senior Educator at Valley Beth Shalom in Encino, California, where he both served as a pulpit rabbi and headed its schools and educational programs. In addition to his work at Valley Beth Shalom, Rabbi Steinberg simultaneously worked toward a doctorate in education at the Jewish Theological Seminary, taught Jewish philosophy in the Graduate School of Education at American Jewish University, and served on local and national boards.

He is a native of Tucson, Arizona, and is the father of three daughters.